40 SUCCESS BUTTONS
and
THE RISE OF
THE EAGLE CHRISTIAN
and
70 THINGS GOD HATES

A MOTIVATIONAL BOOK

FOR SUCCESS.

40 Success Buttons

and

THE RISE of

THE EAGLE CHRISTIAN

and

70 Things God Hates

JEMIMA ALARA

 www.trafford.com
North America & international
toll-free: 1 888 232 4444 (USA & Canada)
fax: 812 355 4082

Contents

Dedication

To Pastor Enoch Adeboye (Daddy G. O)
And
Pastor Mrs Foluke Adeboye (Mummy G.O)
of
The Redeemed Christian Church of God. Daddy and Mummy your exemplary dedicated, faithful and commited life to God and his Church has touched the lives of many people globally. Thank you Daddy and Mummy for your prayers, without which I would'nt have made it.

BOOK ONE

40 SUCCESS BUTTONS

JEMIMA ALARA

__Introduction__

__WHAT IS SUCCESS.__

Success has no universal definition as the parameters for measuring success differs, from person to person. To some success is measured in terms of monetary wealth, that is being able to achieve financial independence and abundant prosperity.

To some others success is measured in terms of academic, career or political heights.

To some others success is when they are able to achieve a particular goal that they have set for themselves in any sphere of their life, which could be buying a new house, passing an exam, winning a gold medal and so on.

In Christendom, success is being able to fulfill your God given assignment, being able to live out God's blue print for your life, the Zoe life, the super abundant life, the life of having a perfect relationship with God, and being right in the center of God's perfect will for your life.

To some others success is fulfilling your potentials, living your dreams and having the ability to maximize your potentials to the fullest. An example was, Mother

Theresa of Calacuta. She was not rich, but she was very successful and she left an undeniable mark and her footprints on the sands of time. She lived her dream of helping the poor, disadvantaged and the less privileged to the best she could. Also the Wright brother's who invented the airplane lived their dreams of inventing an aircraft that could carry people in the skies. That to them was success.

"Success is achieved by ordinary people with an extraordinary determination.

Zig Ziglar.

Over all success can be seen as an act you do or a path you follow that results in a desired goal.

Also the intriguing thing about success is that, no one can do it for you, you are the sole determinant of whether you want to be successful or not. It is a personal decision and choice.

Also you do not sit down all day, daydreaming and wishing for success without doing nothing. Just as faith without works is dead, so wishful thinking without works will not produce success. What produces success are the right steps you are ready to undertake and sacrifices you are willing to make.

There is no shortcut to success, but there are roadmaps to success. With the right information in your hands, you can activate success. Therefore in your hands lies this wonderful book which contain 40 steps that will guide as a roadmap and put you on the right track to achieve success. Rise up and challenge yourself with these steps and see every button you press responding favourably in your favour.

SEE YOU AT THE TOP.

(1)

THE LAW OF DISCOVERY.

"For with you is the fountain of life, in your light we see light."

Psalm 36 v 9.

The first key to success, is to discover who you are. Who are you? Who made you? Why are you existing? Why are you on this earth? What is this world about? Where is your source? Where did you originate from? Where are you heading to? And a whole lot of questions.

Now the moment you start thinking this way, then you have set the ball rolling in the right direction, because discovery leads to revelation and revelation brings illumination (light) and illumination drives away ignorance.

And when light comes darkness/ignorance disappears. Revelation will give you understanding and empower you. How do you get revelation as a Christian? To get revelation you need the manual which is the book of life, the HOLY BIBLE.

Every manufacturer always includes a manual in every product it produces. The purpose of the manual is to provide you with the necessary information you need to know regarding the product you just purchased. It would also give you instructions on how to use the product and make it function according to the intent of the manufacturer. Also the manual contains information about the manufacturer, such as who the manufacturer is, the telephone number and necessary contact details.

For instance if you buy a brand new television or a handset, the manual would give you instructions on how to use it and make it function properly. The manual would tell you all about the product, and in case you are faced with any problems you would quickly refer to the manual for further instructions and if the problem persists you would get in touch with the manufacturer. In this case every human being is a product of God and God is the manufacturer.

"So God created man in his own image, in the image of God he created him, male and female he created them."
Genesis 1 v 27.

You are the clay and God is the potter that moulded you. As a product of God, God has given us his manual which is the word of God (Bible). The bible contains all the information we need to know such as who we are, what product we are made of and how we can function properly in this world to be in accordance with the intent of God. The bible reveals the mind of God who is our manufacturer, concerning us the product. Also the purpose of every product is determined in the factory and not in the market. So to find our purpose we need to get back to our source, our maker. We can never find our purpose in the market. The market referred here, symbolically represents and stands for this present world we live in. That is why most people get it wrong. The world is polluted, lies in darkness and the devil is the god of this world. So tell me, how can the stupid devil who has been judged and is doomed for everlasting destruction define your purpose for you.

Therefore it is time for christians to readdress their steps and go back to the factory and seek the face of God to know their real purpose why they are created. Take a fish out of water and it can't function, take a man out of God and he can't be the best. If you want to be at your best elements then get back to basics, get back to Eden, back to your source, your maker to find out and learn what stuff you are made off. Also the bible is our spiritual mirror where our true identity of who we are is revealed unto us. Also the word of God illuminates our life and directs our ways in life.

Thy word is a lamp unto my feet and a light for my path.
Ps 119 v 105.

Without the manual you would never be able to discover who you are or know the mind of God concerning you and you would also wade through life, without the knowledge of God your maker.

Our Lord Jesus Christ fulfilled his mission here on earth because he was able to discover his purpose when he located what was written about him in Luke 4 v 17 - 21.

On the sabbath day Jesus went into the synagogue and the scroll of the prophet Isaiah was handed to him. **Unrolling it, he found the place where it was written about him.**

After Jesus found what was written about him, his earthly ministry began and he fulfilled everything that was contained in the scroll. Beloved there is something powerful about **THE LAW OF DISCOVERY AND UNTIL YOU DISCOVER YOUR PURPOSE, LIFE IS MEANINGLESS AND REDUCED TO A BURDEN.** God designed every human being uniquely because despite the billions of people here on earth, no two human beings have the same finger prints. Everybody has his or her own unique fingerprint, therefore you are unique and you have a purpose here on earth, rise up and discover it. Beloved there is something written about you and you have to open the book (bible) yourself to discover it. No one can do this for you.

Also according to Smith Wigglesworth, a very great healing evangelist who was used mightily by God to perform extra-ordinary miracles, where the dead were raised back to life, the blind saw, the lame walk, the sick got healed and so on, had this to say regarding the bible,

The bible is the word of God, supernatural in origin external in duration, inexpressible in valor, infinite in scope, regenerative in power, infallible in authority, universal in interest, personal in application, inspired in totality.
Read it through, write it down, pray it in, work it out and then pass it on. Truly it is the word of God. It brings into man the personality of God, it changes the man until he becomes the epistle of God.

It transforms his mind, changes his character, takes him on from grace to grace and gives him an inheritance in the spirit. God comes in, dwells in, walks in, talks through and sups with him.

Smith Wigglesworth.

Also the fear of God is the beginning of wisdom and knowledge of the holy one understanding. Proverbs 9 v 10.

The knowledge of God would give you wisdom, knowledge and understanding. The bible would guide you throughout life, it will also navigate your way in life and lead you into the glorious destiny designed by God exclusively for you. In other words the bible can be likened to a SAT- NAV, whereby all you do is just to type in your destination and it will direct you all the way, until you reach your final destination effortlessly. Friends enough of beating about the bush, it is time to get to basics and hook up to the manufacturer. The bible will give you vital information on how to live a worthy and pleasing life unto God. A life lived which does not please God is a wasted life. We should endeavour to make the bible our companion every time. All that you need to excel in life is in the bible.

Joshua 1 v 8 states *"This book of the law shall not depart out of your mouth, but you shall meditate on it day and night, that you may observe and do according to all that is written in it. For then you shall make your way prosperous, and then you shall deal wisely and have GOOD SUCCESS."*

Look no further, God is all you need to have your needs met and to live a fulfilled life. Isaiah 60 v 2 states that, darkness covers the earth and thick darkness is over the people. Friends, you need the light of God to shine in this dark world. God is light and he would only shine on you if you fear him and keep his commandments.

John Rockefeller a man who rose out of poverty to stardom and great wealth was one man that feared and obeyed the commandment of God. Right from the tender age of 16, he started tithing, and he taught bible studies well over 20 years and God blessed him tremendously. Today, even in death his total worth stands at 340 billion dollars and it keeps increasing. This is what he had to say regarding the bible,
And we are never too old to study the bible. Each time the lessons are studied comes new meaning, some new thought which will make us better.

John Rockefeller.

Also Abraham Lincoln one of the finest president America ever produced had this to say,

I believe the bible is the best gift God has ever given to man. All the good from the saviour of the world is communicated to us through this book.

Abraham Lincoln.

You can't shine with darkness hovering over you. Very importantly you should also understand that this shining we are talking about is not restricted to this world only, but your shinning shines forever into eternity and you would reign with Christ forever and ever.

Furthermore the whole essence of this life, that is the whole reason why you were created and existing on this planet earth, has been summarised by King Solomon, the wisest man that ever lived in,

Ecclesiastes 12 v 13 "All has been heard, the end of the matter is, fear God (revere and worship him, knowing that he is)
And keep his commandments, for this is the whole of man (the full, original purpose of his creation, the object of Gods providence, the root character, the foundation of all happiness, the adjustment to all in harmonious circumstances and conditions under the sun)
and the whole duty for every man."(Amplified bible.)

(2)

RENEW YOUR THINKING.

Do not conform any longer to the pattern of this world, but be transformed by the renewing of your mind.

Romans 12 v 2.

The quest for success starts from the head, from your thoughts, it is all borne in the mind. If you don't change your thinking you can't change your life. This is a statement of truth and not facts. You have to think success, to get success.

You need to have an achievers mentality, to achieve anything in life. Hear this the only reason why people, mostly Christians fail to achieve success is simply due to having a wrong mindset. The engine room of your life is your mind, therefore it is your responsibility to renew your mind in order to achieve great heights of success. One general notion about successful people is that their mindset has been sterotyped to always think success. And they do this first, way before success comes to them. It is so simple, yet most people seem to miss it.

The word of God says it all in Romans 12 v 2 and Joshua 1 v 8. It admonishes us that if we want to transform our lives, we have to renew our minds. Friends without renewing your minds, the status quo remains the same. You can be a christian for as long as you want, but if you fail to renew your mind to align with God's word, success will be far from you.

But if you don't get your mind renewed with these bible facts even though you are born again or filled with the Holy Spirit and speak in tongues, you will remain a negative person and miss the blessing of God.

Kenneth Copeland.

This statement was made by Kenneth Copeland a man who rose out of abject poverty and ignorance of God, to become one of the most successful, wealthy and God fearing minister of God, in the world today.

Now lets us go back to the garden of Eden to really understand what this thought process is all about. Adam was the first man to be created and by all ramifications he was the most successful man that ever lived. Till date, no one has beaten his record of success. Adam was simply an epitome of success, he had everything at his disposal, he was in charge of everything God had created.

Adam had dominion, power, authority and everything under heaven and earth were under his control. He could command the birds of the air, the animals, he could speak to the plants and he was in full control of the earth. He lived in supernatural abundance, he lived a Zoe lifestyle. The pinnacle of his success was heightened by the fact that he had a perfect relationship with God, he could see God, talk with God one on one, he could walk side by side with God, infact he was more or less like God's personal assistant, because he gave names to all what God created and he was right in the center of God's will for his life. Adam was living out success in his place of destiny, his place of purpose and place of perfect location exclusively designed solely for him, untill there came a shift.

After the fall, Adam lost his place of destiny, he lost success and was defeated, he was de -promoted to the lower base life. Now let us examined what happened. **What really happened was that, as a result of the fall there was an immediate shift, an immediate switch in the thinking of Adam.** Adam suddenly become reprobate in his thinking, his thinking immediately twisted to the opposite direction and all he could think of was negativity, fear, defeat, insecurity, hopelessness, shame and all sorts.

His thinking told him he was naked, his thoughts told him to hide from God and he went into hiding, he became fearful, ashamed, timid and he desperately needed to cover himself. From all this, we can deduce that his thoughts changed dramatically.

What happened to this man that could see God, commune with God, chat with God, walk hand in hand with God suddenly all he wanted to do was to hide from God, he no longer felt bold to do the things he used to do with God. He felt seperated. God never drove him away, or scolded him, but rather when he heard God he decided to ran from God.

And the man and his wife heard the sound of the Lord God as he was walking in the garden in the cool of the day, and they hid from the Lord God among the trees of the garden. But the Lord God called to the man, where are you.

Genesis 3 v 8.

So we can see that it all starts from the head, from the mind of reasoning. Adam's reasoning led him to do all that stuff. However Jesus came to restore man back to his original location, and to reposition man back to the place of success, back to victory, back to being in the center of Gods perfect will, back to the way Adam's thinking was before the fall and back to having that perfect relationship with God which guarantees success. God wants our thoughts to be kingdom based, to think the way heaven wants us to think, to think success and never defeat, to think like Jesus.

So therefore you would start enjoying success from the day you are able to finally renew your mind to align with God's words and you start living out the original purpose of God for your life. **Jesus died so that everyone can have access to renew their minds and enjoy great success.**

Friends, the adamic unregenerated mind will limit you forever, but the mind that is renewed and transformed by the word of God will take you places. Amen.

You can't change your life, if you don't change your thinking. And you can't walk in your full potentials to maximise success, if you don't renew your mind to conform to Gods word.

The children of Israel, despite all the miraculous signs they witnessed, they still refused to renew their minds and think the way God wanted them to think. And when it was time to cross over into the promised land, their thinking made them to back pedal and most of them never got into their inheritance. They thought of defeat and not success and because of this wrong thinking, defeat it became for them and they lost out. Friends to enjoy success, You must be ready to change your thinking to conform and align with God's word. The word of God has the power to realign anything that has been misaligned in your life.

Be transformed by the renewing of your minds.
(Rom 12 v 2)

So it all starts in the mind.
Also every child of God has the DNA of success inside of them, but this DNA will lie dormant until it is activated and the way to activate this is by renewing your mind to conform and align with God's word. For we walk by faith (that is by the word of God) and not by sight (that is not by what we see).
We achieve great heights of success by faith and not in the human flesh or by sight.

(3)

HAVE A DREAM/VISION FOR YOURSELF.

"And Joseph had a dream."

Genesis 37 v 5.

"And Joseph had another dream."

Genesis 37 v 9.

Some call it dream, some call it vision, whichever way you choose to call it, it has one and the same definition. You do not have to necessarily fall asleep like Joseph and have a dream, but you can be right awake and have a dream/vision. A dream or a vision is how you want to see yourself in the nearest future, say 2, 5, or 10 years time, what do you want to see happen in your life by then.

With vision the power of imagination comes into play. You conceive an idea through your imagination, the result of that idea is what is called a vision.

All achievement has a beginning with an idea.
Napoleon Hill.

A man's greatness lies in the power of thought.
Myles Munroe.

Idea is the strongest currency in business market.
David Oyedepo.

Also it is very important not only to keep your dream alive, but you must also ensure to live your dream. Joseph had a dream and he held unto this dream, he kept the dream alive, he lived his dream and he held unto his dream, despite all the trials he went through.

He had faith that one day his dreams will surely come to pass. His dream kept his hopes up and gave him the will power to endure all the hardship he went through. Therefore you must ensure you have a dream/vision. Your dream will keep you going, and enable you to stay afloat when you face challenges and trials. Life is too precious to be lived at aimlessly, without a definite direction. If you don't aim for something, you would aim at nothing and fall for anything.

If you can dream it, you can do it.
Walt Disney.

Dreams are powerful and they have potentials to live on. Example is Martin Luther King. Martin Luther King had a dream, he did not keep it to himself but he shared it with the whole world because he believed that one day his dream will come to pass. And he publically kept declaring it boldly. He kept on saying,
I have a dream that one day my four children will one day live in a nation, where they will not be judged by the colour

of their skin, but the content of their character. Also where there will be equality, without any racial discrimination, no black, no white.

Although at that time he was declaring it, it looked absolutely impossible, but he kept at it. And many years later, not only have we witnessed equality in America, but we have a black man (Barrack Obama) who was duly elected as the president of America. Please note that majority of Americans are white and they all voted for him, for two terms.

Friends never you under estimate your dreams and also note that no one can dream for you, it is a personal decision that has to be undertaken absolutely by you yourself.

Also you can't hit a goal or target if you are not aiming at one. Having a vision for your life, portrays you as a serious minded person. Vision defines your direction in life. Most Christians lack vision for their lives, when you ask them, what their vision for life is, some would say they are still praying, six months, one year, two years and they are still praying. Others would say they are waiting on God, meanwhile God is waiting for them to act. Others would say "Well let's see what God would do", others would quote the maxim QUI SERA, SERA, meaning whatever would be, would be. Others would say, you know I am still praying and watching and waiting. The excuses never ends.

It is a terrible thing to see and have no vision.

Helen Keller.

Beloved God has deposited everything in you, everything you need to succeed, it's now left for you to unleash your God given potentials. You need to have a vision for your life. You can't fold your arms and keep watching and waiting. As a child of the Most High God, no one can stop you from realising your vision, except yourself.

You are the only one to stop yourself, not even the devil and all his demonic angels can stop you. God has given us authority over all the powers of darkness and the stupid devil. (Luke 10 v 19).

Furthermore "For with God nothing shall be impossible."

In Genesis 11 v 1-8, the people of the earth gathered and IMAGINED within themselves to build a city and a tower to reach heaven. They had a VISION of living in a city that reaches to the sky.

And they swung straight into action by living the dream and they started taking steps to bring the dream into actual realisation. They did not just sit down, fold their arms and daydream. No, they lived the dream and took steps to fulfil it.

If you have a vision and you don't act on it, it will die.
Benson Idahosa.

And this is what God had to say in;

Genesis 11 v 6 "And the Lord said, behold they are one people and they all have one language and this is the beginning of what they will do, and NOW NOTHING

THEY HAVE IMAGINED TO DO WILL BE IMPOSSIBLE FOR THEM."

From the above scripture, we see God affirming the power of vision.

For your vision, you need to first of all, use the power of your imagination, the power of your thoughts. Engage your mind positively.

Every star is known to be a thinker and every committed thinker is bound to be a star.

David Oyedepo.

After imagining your vision, you have to write it down, this is compulsory and the scripture below confirms that.

"Write the vision and make it plain on tablets, so that a herald (that is you) may run (not sleep or daydream) with it."
Habakkuk 2 v 2. Emphasis added.

Regarding writing down vision, recently i was having a chat with a seven year old girl, called Miss Tomi, and we were talking about what she hoped for in life, i encouraged her to dream big and she said a lot of mind blowing things she wanted to achieve in life. After talking for a while, she told me she had said enough. I said O. K. And we shifted the topic, after about five minutes interval she requested for a paper and a pen, i asked her what she needed it for, she told me she wanted to write down all she had said and use it as reference. I was so bewildered at such display of wisdom coming out of a seven year old child. Meanwhile there are a lot of adults who don't even have a dream, and those who have dreams don't see it as a necessity to write it down in order to be able to run with it.

After writing down your vision, you need to set a time frame for yourself, because
"Every vision is yet for an appointed time, it speaks of the end." Habakkuk 2 v 3.

"Also surely there is an end and the expectation of the righteous shall not be cut off." Proverbs 23 v18

For instance Mr A has a vision of becoming a medical doctor. Now that is a good vision, and he has to attach a time frame for achieving this. He has to begin running with that vision, by taking steps and not just sit down and daydream.

A life without vision is very precarious and it can be likened to a sailor setting out on a voyage without a specific destination in mind. That sailor would just be tossed here and there by the winds of life and would keep going round and round.

According to Myles Munroe (one of the finest men of God, our generation ever saw) says that the poorest person on earth is a man without a vision.

He also goes further and says that the greatest tragedy on earth is not death, but it is a life lived without a vision and without a clear defined purpose.

A man with a vision is a man with a purpose, and is a man on a mission, who has his eyes fixed and such a man can't be swayed about easily.

Also very importantly it is never too late to have a vision. You can start, right now.

Create the highest, grandest vision possible for your life, because you become what you believe.

Oprah Winfrey.

(4)

EFFECTIVE PLANNING.

"Suppose one of you wants to build a tower. Will he not first sit down and estimate the cost to see if he has enough money to complete it."

Luke 14 v 28.

Most Christians lack the ability to plan. As a Christian you do not just fold your arms and wade through life with a "WHAT WILL BE, OR LET IT BE ATTITUDE."

A productive life is not by accident.
Myles Munroe.

Things don't just happen, things are made to happen.
John Kennedy.

If you leave your life to chance, you don't have a chance.
David Oyedepo.

Also you do not loaf around and wait for manna to drop from heaven. No, it does not work that way anymore.

The days of Manna dropping from heaven is long over. This time around you have to rise up and be effective, and God has promised to bless the work of your hands.

Friends, there is no short cut to success, but there are roadmaps to success. For instance Mr A is seeking for an employment, he sleeps at 9pm and wakes up the following day at 10am. He reads his bible for another 2hrs, then watches T.V and laze around for another 8 hours and finally goes to bed at 9pm. Tell me where is the planning.

God would not do for you, what you have to do, God would give you ideas and favour, but then there is your part that you have to play. Mr A has to get up, polish his shoes, dress well, prepare a good curriculum vitae (C V), search for potential companies and then send in his application letters. After he has done all he has to do, then he can now back it up with prayer and fasting and then watch God move mightily on his behalf.

In Genesis 11 v 1-8 the people had a vision of building a tower, they did not loaf around, but they started planning towards their vision by moulding bricks and mortar.

To be successful in life you need to plan effectively, if you do not plan at anything or for anything you are likely to fail. Jesus gave a parable that a man building a house would first of all sit down and plan. A jump into the river without first of all, testing the depths of the waters is very dangerous.

When you stop planning and preparing you stop winning.
Zig Ziglar.

In everything you do, adequate preparation is very essential. You need to plan and be prepared well ahead of time. This saves cost and time. A farmer prepares for farming season well ahead of time. He starts planning during the harvest season and does not wait till the planting season. If he waits for the planting season, before planning he is bound to fail because there would be no prepared seed to plant, therefore he can't expect any harvest.

Most times we blame the devil, but some Christians are the enemies of themselves and the architect of their own problems. According to Myles Munroe, he says that some of the laziest people are Christians, they expect God to do everything for them. God can not resist the devil for you, God has given you the tools to use to resist the devil, so it is up to you. If you resist the devil he would surely flee, but if you become slothful and leave things to chance, then you have yourself to blame. Also you are giving the devil open door access into your life, because you just don't want to do anything and not wanting to do anything could be seen as gambling. Children of God don't gamble.

So therefore rise up and plan.

You don't need a century to effect a change, you only need effective preparation to provoke unusual transformation.
David Oyedepo.

Our Lord Jesus Christ did not walk the surface of this earth aimlessly. No, Jesus had a plan, he knew where he should be and what he should be doing at any given time. He planned for everything, right from the moment he came back from the wilderness, to the washing of the disciples feet, to the triumphant entry on the back of the colt, till the last supper, up until the last prayer at the garden of Gethsemane. Jesus had it all laid out.

By failing to prepare, you are preparing to fail.
Benjamin Franklin.

When you plan, you become in charge of situations and not the situation taking charge over you. For years David planned the building of the temple of God little by little, and his son Solomon at the end of the day, built the temple and the temple was not only well built but it was very magnificent and very beautiful.

(5)

STRATEGY

People aren't going to show up at your front door and make your dreams come true.

Donald Trump

You have a vision, you have a plan. The question is how do you make it happen? How do you realise or achieve your vision. It is this line of thoughts that is called strategy. How do you move to get to your destination/goal. How do you move from point one to point two, from A to B, what would it take, what is involved. It is like a game of chess, taking strategic steps and moves.

Strategy is like a conveyor belt that will carry your VISION + PLANS into actual realisation. Without effective strategy, you could be stuck without knowing why. Please do not miss this step but spend considerable amount of time strategizing your moves.

In Genesis 11 v 1-8 "The people of the earth had a vision of building a city whose top would reach the skies, then they went ahead and planned towards it by building bricks and mortar, after that they adopted a strategy towards achieving their vision and that was, they all had to come together, they had to be united before they can build.

Now let us examine the above scripture closely, The people from inception,

1) Had a VISION of building a city whose top would reach the sky.

2) And they also had an EFFECTIVE PLAN. I use the term effective because they did not plan and go to sleep, but they planned and acted upon their plan by moulding blocks and bricks.

3) The third thing, they did was to STRATEGISE (strategy) on how to realise their vision. And this strategy was that they all had to be united as one in order to build. Their STRATEGY WAS UNITY.

Here we can see VISION + EFFECTIVE PLANNING+ STRATEGY, at play, the three together would surely equal to SUCCESS.

And this strategy was so effective that God had to come down and stop them. And this is what the Almighty God said in;

Genesis 11 v 6 "And the Lord said, behold they are one people and they all have one language and this is the beginning of what they will do, and now NOTHING

THAT HAVE IMAGINED TO DO WILL BE IMPOSSIBLE FOR THEM."

These people were simply unstoppable and their success would have been 100% guaranteed. It took only the Almighty God to stop them and no one else.

In the book of Esther chapter 3, there was a decree set out to annihilate all the Jews on a particular date. When Mordecai and the Jews heard about the decree, they immediately took a decision that they were going to live and not die.

Friends, that decision of choosing to live and refusing to die is what can be referred to as a vision or a dream. They dreamt of life, not death.

Now what next? Because you do not have a vision and just fold your arms and do nothing. No, you are to run with it until it comes to pass.

So that a herald (that is you) may run with it.
Habakkuk 2 v 2b.

Now this is what they did, from the time the decree of death was passed,

1) They imagined life and not death. (VISION)
2) They decided on an action plan and that was to approach the king to cancel the decree and Queen Esther was the only appropriate person to do this. (EFFECTIVE PLANNING).

However with this plan came an obstacle, and that was anyone who approached the king without an invitation had only one punishment and that was death. Now Esther had not yet been invited to approach the king.

Friends sometimes, you would face obstacles and barriers on the way to fulfil your dreams. It would not be an easy smooth ride all the time, but wither which way, you have to pursue your dreams.

Do not allow anything to hinder you, shove every obstacle aside and press on, move on, run with your vision.

The Jews did not allow this obstacle to hinder them at all and they moved on.

3) Now they have a VISION, they have A PLAN, and they need a conveyor belt to get them to their destination in order to realise their dream of staying alive. Now this is when, STRATEGY comes into play. What strategy should they adopt?

They must have put their thinking caps on and glory be to God, because after much consultation and deliberation among themselves the Jews had a hindsight that this vision OF STAYING ALIVE could only be achieved on the platform of spiritual warfare (that is through prayer and fasting) and not on a physical platform (naturally in the flesh).

Friends sometimes we need the platform of spiritual warfare, for our dreams to be fulfilled. The realm of the spirit exist for real, and the word of God confirms this in Ephesians 6 v 12, For we wrestle not against flesh and blood, but against the rulers, against the authorities, against spiritual forces of evil in the heavenly realms.

And also note, that we do not wage war as the world wages war, for the weapons of our warfare are not carnal, they are not physical weapons. One of the weapons of our warfare is Prayer.

And Jesus confirmed this in Mark 9 v 29 and said this kind does not go except by prayer and fasting.

That means there are some type of obstacles to fulfilling your dreams, that would not go, until you attack it spiritually through prayer and fasting.

FOR MORE ON SPIRITUAL WARFARE, I WOULD RECOMMEND YOU READ MY BOOK TITLED **"YOUR SPIRITUAL AUTHORITY."**

So the Jews adopted the STRATEGY of spiritual warfare, they swung into action and Queen Esther called a fast, she instructed all the Jews not to eat and drink anything for three days and three nights including herself and after that she would approach the king. What wisdom, they fought this battle spiritually. And in the end the Jews prevailed and their vision of staying alive was realised. Also they did not only live, but they also lived in style and affluence because, they ruled over their enemies and the fear of them fell over all the inhabitants of that region, both far and wide.

Every true child of God has all what it takes to succeed. We have the seed of greatness on our inside. We have the DNA of our God on our inside. "Greater is he that is in us than he that is in the world." 1st John 4 v 4.

Also the word of God says in 1st Corinthians 2 v 9 "Eyes have not seen, no ear has heard, no mind has conceived what God has prepared for those who love him."

Whoa! what more proof do we need? It is time to arise, shake off every complacency and embark on an effective strategy to bring all your dreams to pass and live life to the fullest. Amen.

(6)

SET GOALS FOR YOURSELF.

Give me a stock clerk with a goal and i will give you a man who will make history. Give me a man without a goal and i will give you a stock clerk.

J C Penny.

There is nothing as powerful as having clear cut goals. Clear cut goals gives you precision and clarity of purpose in the journey of life. It makes you more effective, focused and streamlines your path in life. For instance, every product has a purpose / a goal. A footballers goal is to win almost every match. A fisherman's goal is to catch as many fishes as possible. The goal of every athlete is to win the gold. The goal of every lawyer is to win every case. So then, what's your goal?

Goal setting is very important in everything you do in life. If you don't raise the roof in your life, by setting up goals and standards in your life, you can hardly achieve anything. Achievers are those who set goals and see to it that they get them accomplished.

A goal is a dream with a deadline.

Napoleon Hill.

The more they achieve the more they raise the goals up. No successful man or woman wakes up in the day, without knowing what to do for that day. They know exactly what they want done or achieved every minute, every hour, every day, every month, every year and so on. If you don't set goals, you are simply gambling with time. Make every day count, by doing something that will bring you towards your goals.

When you set goals for yourself, you achieve a lot. Setting goals is like placing a task on yourself on a daily, weekly or monthly basis. The human nature is such that if we do not put ourselves in check, we tend to become complacent as time goes by.

One area of concern to everyone in the body of Christ is the issue of our flesh "MR FLESH". Mr flesh is nobody's friend and it would always try to get in the way. But it is our responsibility to keep it under control, keep it in check always. For instance when you want to pray, MR FLESH would want to sleep, when you want to fast, MR FLESH wants to eat. What do you do? Would you give in to MR FLESH? That is why you have to set goals, because if you know you have to fast and pray and MR FLESH wants to eat and sleep, you would simply say no, because you have a target to achieve your goals for that day or season.

Galatians 5 v 17 says it all,
For the sinful nature desires what is contrary to the spirit, and the spirit what is contrary to the sinful nature. They are in conflict with each other.

Also apostle Paul in the book of Rom 7 v 14 - 24 had this to say also regarding MR. FLESH, he said that he brings his body into subjection. That is he deals with his flesh on a daily basis. He controls his flesh and does not allow it to get in the way of his spiritual life.

So on a daily basis in order to keep up with the Spirit, I recommend you set goals for yourself. Set a timetable for yourself and include different times when you would do specific things. Include times, such as when to have your quiet time, work schedule for the day, tea time, break time, prayer time, bible study time and also how many chapters of the bible you are to read every day, and so on.

You have to ensure, you follow this strictly, by so doing you are not only growing in the Lord and achieving a lot, but you are also keeping your flesh in check, so that your flesh does not misbehave and thereby acts as a hindrance to your growth.

But if you do not have a checklist, no goal setting, you would be a man or woman without control or checks. And anything silly or frivolous would gladly occupy your time. Also note the saying goes, that an idle mind is the devil's workshop.

Also because there is no checks and balances on your time, at the time when you are supposed to memorise bible verses, you would gladly engage in gossiping or frivolity.

Also there is no restraint, no yardstick to measure whether you are maturing both spiritually and physically if you don't set goals for yourself.

For instance, let us take this scenario of Mr A's goal setting in one year, (Year 1),

1. To read through the whole bible twice.
2. To increase his wealth by 20%.
3. To win 10 souls to the kingdom of God and make sure they are firmly planted in the house of God.
4. To go on prison visits.
5. To wait on the Lord in prayer and fasting three times every month.

Now because Mr A, has set these goals for himself, he has been able to have a definite plan and programme for himself and throughout the year and he would work so hard to fulfil all of them. At the end of the year Mr A, is happy because he has achieved everything.

Now Mr A looks forward to the next coming year with great joy, and it is time for him once again, to set new goals. Now Mr A has yardstick for which to use to set new goals for himself in the coming year. (Year 2).

Now he has to step up with his goals, he has to challenge himself, because he can't do exactly what he did last year.

If he does that, that would amount to stagnancy. No one wants to be stagnant, so in order to avoid being on the same spot he has to move up, now the appropriate goal he would set for the new year would probably look like this;

1. To read through the bible at least four times.
2. To increase his wealth by say 30 - 40%.
3. To win at least 15- 20 souls to God.
4. To increase prison visit and also include hospital visits.
5. To wait on the Lord in a fast up to five to seven times a month.
6. To go on a personal retreat to spend time with God for 2 weeks twice in the year.
7. To memorize three bible verses every day.

Now we can see that Mr A is going to achieve more in the coming year, he is also growing both spiritually and physically. That is how God expects all his children to grow. Now if Jesus tarries, in the third year Mr A would step up higher and higher with each coming year.

Now assuming Mr A had not imbibed the culture of setting goals for himself and he takes each year casually as it comes, Mr A would not be able to ascertain his progress, he would not know whether he is growing or retarding spiritually, because there is nothing to measure up against.

Please setting goals for ourselves is very vital, it is not optional and anyone who loves success must set goals and targets.

Setting goals is the first step in turning the invisible into visible.
Tony Robbins.

You can start doing it on a daily basis, weekly basis, monthly basis or yearly basis. Everyday you check yourself and examine your progress, by so doing you would also be able to drive away any little fox that is trying to ruin your vineyard, but if you do not have a checklist, you would not even know or detect these little foxes and they would grow and be mighty and of course you and I know the consequence.

Now write a to do list for yourself on what you want to achieve or get done daily. Then as you go along the day with each one you get done, you give a tick. Every day you wake up, you must set goals for that day, your success tomorrow starts today and whatever you do today, would reflect in your future. Your future is in your present, this very moment, today and not tomorrow.

Your future depends on what we do in the present,
Mahatma Gandhi.

Life changes only when your daily priorities changes.
Myles Munroe

Beloved, make the most of your day and set goals for yourself, you would be amazed at how much you can achieve.

KEY NOTE.

STEPS TO ACHIEVE YOUR GOAL.

1. Identify the goal (Vision)
2. Organize resources available to achieve the goal. (Planning)
3. Formulate a plan of action. (Strategy.
4. Execute that plan. (Action). For more on Action, please refer to the 33rd success button on page 148.

(7)

DIVINE DIRECTION / GUIDIANCE

"You would hear a voice behind you saying this is the way, walk in it."

Beloved, life can be likened to a journey through a big jungle and if you have a guide, you are very sure of getting to your destination and getting there quickly. Imagine not having a guide, you would just keep going round and round in circles and one is likely to spend life groping in the dark.

Also life can be seen as lots of jigsaw puzzles and you need an expert to fix it up for you. God is not only an expert, he is expert himself, he is the creator of all.

As a Christian, a true child of God, God is your shepherd and you are the sheep, therefore God is committed to guiding you. Every shepherd guides it's sheep. However the question is are you ready to be guided? Are you ready to be a sheep?

"I will instruct you and teach you in the way you should go."
Psalm 32 v 8.

However are you ready to listen out for his voice, do you consult God on any step you are about to take, have you laid your plans before God, do you trust him with all your heart, are you leaning on your own understanding, have you acknowledged him to be your shepherd?

The crucial key to get divine direction is that you have to be willing to become a sheep. God will only guide sheep and not goats, dogs, etc, The bible says My sheep hear and know my voice. God is only a shepherd of sheep. To be a sheep you have to be meek, you have to be willing to be led. You have to be ready to submit to the shepherd. You have to display the fruits of the spirit and not the works of the flesh.

King David was one king who sought the Lord in any decision, he wanted to take, the only few decisions he did not consult God on, resulted in serious calamity. Decisions such as;

1. Taking Uriah's life when he realised Bathsheba was pregnant.
2. Taking a census of the army of Israel.

Beloved going forward determine to make God your shepherd. And in everything you do always put God first and you would never go wrong.

When you put God first, you are assured of divine presence. The divine presence of God will be with you and lead you all through. The divine presence of God was with the Israelites and when the red sea saw them it could not hold together but it had to flee away. Why was it so, because it could not stand the presence of God that was with them.

When Israel came out of Egypt, the house of Jacob from a people of foreign tongue,
The sea looked and fled, the Jordan turned back, the mountains skipped like rams, the hills like lambs.

Ps 114 v 1 - 4

Also the presence of God will go far ahead of you and will sort things out for you well ahead of time, even before your physical presence appears.

I will go before you and will level the mountains. I will break down the gates of bronze and cut through bars of iron.

Isaiah 45 v 2.

Also it does not matter if you have tried to sort it out on your own and in so doing have gotten your fingers burnt, turn it over to God. God would fix it up for you, don't carry on trying to work it out, otherwise you may end up with your whole body burnt as well.

(8)

AIM HIGH

Shoot for the moon. Even if you miss you will land amongst the stars.

Jill Mc Lemore.

Winners always look up, they never look down. To succeed you have to always aim very high. The bottom is always crowded and it is for everybody, always look up because the sky is never crowded. Why is the sky never crowded, because majority of people are not ready to pay the price that would take them to the top.

The book of Genesis 15 gives us a classical example of how God wants us to think. In this passage Abraham was thinking in a very limited way and God had to bring him out of his tent and showed him how to think.

God took him outside and said, Look up at the heavens and count the stars, if indeed you can count them, so shall your offspring be.

Gen 15 v 6.

A tent can be described as an enclosed space. It has a restricted space and when you are in it, you are secluded and confined to a limited space. You can't go beyond or above, all you do has to be confined within the tent. Thinking within your tent will make you base your thoughts on logic and the bible admonishes us not base our thoughts on logic, but to base our thoughts on faith, for we walk by faith and not by sight. Faith will make you take a leap and step out of your tent, out of limitation and human logic and make you think big, think according to God's standards.

For instance in Mark 6 v 30 - 44, when Jesus fed five thousand people with five loaves of bread and two fishes, according to logic this can't be, absolutely impossible but by faith it was possible and there was a left over of 12 baskets after 5000 people had eaten. Whoa. What a mighty God we serve.

Therefore never you think within the confines of your tent anymore, always think high, aim high, high above the skies into the heavens. With the right thinking, Think big, that is the key and the only way. No matter what you do, or regardless of your present circumstances, just aim high by thinking big. Thinking big is the driving force that has forged all the great achievements in modern life. How big you think, determines how big a success you become. Please note you have nothing to lose by thinking big and you have a lot to gain by thinking big, so why not go for it by starting to big. comes great success.

Success will not lower its standard to us. We must raise our standards to success.

Rev Randal Mc Bride Jnr.

It is not where you start, but how high you aim that matters for success.

Nelson Mandela.

☙❧☙❧☙

(9)

BE AN EFFECTIVE MANAGER OF YOUR TIME.

"Lord teach us to number our days."

Ps 90 v 12

Waste your money and you are only out of money, but waste your time and you have lost half of your life.
Micheal Le Boeuf.

Learn to respect time and be a good manager of your time. Whatever you don't respect can't be of any benefit to you. If you respect time it would be of tremendous benefit to you and would yield you great results. You also have to understand that life is in times and seasons, and to everything under the Sun, there is a time and season. A time to be born and a time to die. A time to play and a time to work. (Ecclesiastes 3 v 1 – 8).

Also one equal thing that everyone has is time. There is no disparity, we all have 24 hours in a day. Rich or poor, black or white, famous and infamous, young or old.

Time is capital and God in his infinite mercy has given us all the capital of time on an equal basis, there is no partiality or favouritism. How you use your time, matters a lot and makes a whole lot of difference. If you use your time wisely, you would definitely reap the results.

How do you use your time? One general feature, among successful people who built their business empire from the scratch is that they are not loafers, they hardly sleep. They are effective users of their time. They work around the clock, every second, minute and hour is so precious to them that they do not waste it.

Successful people attach so much value to their time, that you never find them wasting their time mucking about. Friends, you are what you are, due to what you make out of your time. A person who sleeps for more than 12 hours in a day and expects to be successful, is indeed a joker. Please do not get me wrong, sleep is good, but too much of it is bad. Some people just love sleeping, and they can go on marathon sleeping for long hours. This is not productive. No successful person sleeps stupidly. Please do not love sleep.

There is so much to do with your life, so much God has deposited on your inside that sleep would rob you off. You have spent much of your time sleeping when you were a baby, now is the time to grow up and do more with your life.

According to scientist the average human being sleeps for half of their lives. Let us break it down this way, for those who are still moderate and still sleep for just 8 hours a day. Lets us picture such people as Mr A.

1) 8 hours x 7 days = 56 hours.
2) 48 hours gives us two days, so 56 hours will give us 2 and a quarter days.
3) So in a week Mr A sleeps for two and a quarter days.
4) 2 and a quarter days x 4 weeks = 9 days.
5) Therefore in a month Mr A would have slept for 9 days.
6) 9 days x 12 calender months= 108 days.
7) 30 days makes a month, so 108 days will give us 3 months, and 18 days.

So we see that in a year Mr A would have slept for 3 and a half months and four days. Nearly four months.
Whoa, what an absolute waste of time.
Friends this is scary enough, you can now imagine those who have no discipline and can sleep for as long as 10, 12 hours or more.

Beloved, sleep is counter- productive, oh no, please make your life count here on earth. Do not give in to, too much sleep.

The book of Proverbs 20 v 13 admonishes us by charging; "Do not love sleep",

"A little sleep, a little slumber and poverty would come upon you" Proverbs 6 v 10.

Friends, you have in your hands a capital of time, and you are going to give account for it one day. Remember that one day the books would be opened. Some people use their time very well and profitably and some use it foolishly. Please note that in the context of time we are all equal, please attach value to your time, see time as currency and trade wisely with it.

Also to use your time wisely avoid procrastination, by never putting off for later what you can do now. Procrastination is the number one offender against your ability to manage time here.

Also successful entrepreneurs like Richard Branson, Oprah Winfrey, Bill Gates, trade wisely with their time by working around the clock. Show me a successful man, both a believer and an unbeliever, who built a business empire from the scratch and I would tell you without a doubt that such a person attached so much value to their time and made the most out of it.

"All hard work brings profit." Proverbs 14 v 23.

Friends every-day you wake up, you are presented with a beautiful cheque of 24 good hours, please cash this cheque and trade with it wisely by making the best use of your time.

In life there are only 3 ways to describe how time is used. We have those who spend their time, those who while away their time and those who invest their time. Time is money, if you spend money you can't get it back, if you while away your money, by being extravagant you waste it, if you invest your money, you get it back.

Jemima Alara.

Furthermore, to effectively manage your time properly, write a list of targets you want accomplished every hour, every three hours, and so on and at the end of the day, and you would be amazed at how much you can achieve in 24hours.

Also always go to bed each night exhausted and spent with what you have achieved for the day and wake up each day with new targets ready to be accomplished for that day. Your future starts today, right now and not tomorrow.

Also be on the look -out for opportunities. Every-day we are presented afresh with 24 good hours of opportunity, be on the alert and source out opportunities. Please bear in mind that, opportunity always comes disguised, but it would always knock at your door, if you are attentive and timely you would grab it, but if you are not, sadly it would move on to the next available person because *"Time and chance (opportunity) happen to them all"*

Ecclesiastes 9 v 11f.

So you have to be quick to discover opportunities or else time would swallow it up or someone else would see it and quickly grab it.

Don't watch the clock, do what it does, keep going.

Sam levenson.

KEY NOTE ; THE TEN THINGS TO REMEMBER ABOUT TIME.

1) Time can be lost.
2) Time can't be controlled, you can't adjust time, you can't buy time.
3) Time is more important than money.
4) Time can be negotiated like money.
5) Time can be traded like money, it can be revalued and also be devalued.
6) Time can be invested.
7) You can make time your best friend.
8) You can't speed or slow time down.
9) You can use your time to add value to your life.
10) The sum of your life and success depends on how well you use your time.

(10)

BE DILIGENT.

"Do you see a man diligent and skilful in his business, he will stand before kings, he will not stand before obscure men."

Proverbs 22 v 29.

Diligence is doing something very well. In all you do be diligent, even if you are a shoe shiner, shine shoes in an extraordinary way, so much so that your customers would always be on the lookout for you.

In the heart of London there is a particular spot where you have a group of men, they work as team of shoe shiners and they shine shoes so perfectly that you can almost see your face in the shoes. That is diligence. And anytime you pass by, you find top executives, managers, company directors all queuing up to have their shoes polished. Imagine, such a show of diligence.

Furthermore, refine, revise and adopt and work hard everyday to be better than you were yesterday. Soon you will be good. Then you will be great and one day you will be world class.

Friends there is dignity in labour, it does not matter what you do, what matters is how you do it. Do you strive to be excellent in your chosen field or not?

I believe in the dignity of labour. Whether with head or hand, that the world owes no man a living but that it owes everyman an opportunity to make a living.
John D. Rockefeller.

There could be many barbing salons on one street, but it is only the diligent barber that would stand out and shine among the lot. You have to be faithful in little, then God would uplift you to a high level. If you are faithful and diligent in managing that small kiosk, that small kiosk would grow into a chain of mega big stores.

A classical example is the famous Wal mart stores. Samuel Walton the American entrepreneur who founded it was so poor and he started out with one small grocery store and worked so hard to buy another store and then another and the rest is history. Today Wal Mart stores is one of the biggest giant retail stores worldwide, with over 2000 stores, employing over half a million people and clocking an annual sales of over 100 billion US dollars.

Also David's skill of playing the harp made him stand before king Saul. 1st Samuel 16 v 14 – 23.

Diligence and hard work go hand in hand. To be successful there is no single room for laziness but there is a large room for hard work. Without your input of hard work, you cant go far.

Unless you are willing to drench yourself in your work beyond the capacity of the average man you are just not cut out for positions at the top.

J C Penny.

(11)

THE POWER OF PERSEVERANCE.

I do not think there is any other quality so essential to success of any kind as the quality of perseverance, it overcomes almost everything even nature.
John Rockefeller.

Perseverance is a very vital key to success. There is no great story of success without the ingredient of persistence, because life itself is full of ups and downs, life will throw a lot of things at you, but it is your wilful doggedness, continuous tenacity that would keep you going. Majority of people fail to hold their head high above and navigate their boat to beat the tides, but rather they allow the tide of the waters to steer their boat for them. Please bear in mind that the tide is always unfriendly and would continue to toss you about without any clear direction. But you have to take charge and resist the tide by holding on in continuous perseverance.

Before success comes in any mans life, he is sure to meet with much temporary defeat and perhaps some failures. When

defeat overtakes a man, the easiest and most logical thing to do is to quit. That is exactly what the majority of men do.
Napoleon Hill.

Sometime ago in the United States of America, an elderly man who was a retiree had nothing but a simple well prepared chicken recipe. He owned a little restaurant which was leading nowhere. He decided to sell his recipe to restaurant owners who will give him a percentage in return. He drove around the country sleeping in his car, trying to find someone who would back him. He kept knocking on doors and was rejected one thousand and nine times (1009). But he PERSEVERED and finally something miraculous happened and someone said yes to him. This man is no other than Colonel Sanders the founder of Kentucky fried chicken (KFC).

Due to his continuous perseverance he was able to build a multi million business empire at the age of 61 years. Today he is very rich, famous and his name is a trademark all over the world. He had heard the word NO over a thousand times, but he kept on persisting, even in the midst of rejection, disappointment, opposition, difficulties and so on.

This is just one case study, there are several other testimonies of successful people who went through the same process of perseverance. No matter what you are going through, never give up because winners don't quit and quitters don't win.

The word perseverance originally comes from the Latin word Perseverantia, which means to abide by something strictly. This makes sense because if you remain dogged, tenacious and determined in the midst of difficulties and opposing circumstances then you are really being strict with yourself. To reach your goal you have to persevere.

Its not where you start or even what happens to you along the way that's important, what is important is that you persevered and never gave up on yourself.

Zig Ziglar.

Victory belongs to the most persevering.

Napoleon Hill.

Success is the child of drudgery and perseverance. It cannot be coaxed or bribed, pay the price and it is yours.

Orison Sweft Marden.

෧෨෨෨෨

(12)

NEVER DWELL ON THE PAST.

"This one thing I do, forgetting what is behind and straining toward what is ahead, I press on.
Philippians 3 v 13 – 14.

Friends in life you would do yourself a whole lot of good if you can put the past behind you and move ahead.

To design the future effectively you must first let go of your past.

Charles J. Givens.

Take control of your future by letting go of the past. The past is gone forever and no matter what you do, you can't draw back the hands of the clock. Always looking back is a sheer waste of time, because you cant go back that way again, the only way is to move forward, so therefore shut the door to yesterday and embrace the door to your future.

The past has nothing good to offer. Your future is in your present and not your past. Dwelling on your past would not bring any healing. There is no athelete who runs and ever looks back, everyone's eye's is looking towards the finishing line.

Therefore we as Christians are on the race track, we are running a race and we are to look towards Jesus the author and finisher of our faith. There is a prize awaiting you, a glorious crown, which can be missed if you keep looking behind you. Looking back makes you lose focus, please do not take your eyes off Jesus, as long as Peter was looking straight towards Jesus, he walked on water, but the moment he took his eyes off Jesus, he began to sink.

Friends you can blame everyone for your past, but you can never blame anyone for your future, your future is entirely your responsibility. Your future is in your hands. Apostle Paul was a good example, he never dwelt on his past life of Judaism, rather this is what he had to say when he was nearing the end, "I have robbed no one, killed no one.

He saw himself a new man, to him his past never existed, so are we supposed to be, we all have marred past, withered hands, but God has come to give us beauty for ashes, joy for mourning, why do we still want to hold on to the ashes when God has given us beauty.

The past should be the past, dwelling on to the past can destroy the future. Live for what tomorrow has to offer, not for what yesterday has taken away.

Today offers you the opportunity to make good choices, the past is gone and you can only redeem the bad choices of yesterday, by making good choices today, now.

Very importantly 3 helpful ways of breaking of the past is by doing the following,

(1). STOP BLAMING YOURSELF FOR PAST MISTAKES.--If we all could see the future, no one would make any mistake. But we can't see future, therefore we are all bound to make mistakes, so why should you keep blaming yourself. If you keep blaming yourself you are inviting frustration and this will lead to despair, hopelessness, sickness and a whole lot. The world is yet to see anyone who lived without making any mistake. Jesus Christ was the only perfect human being that ever lived. No one is perfect, so stop the blame game.

(2). STOP LIVING IN SELF CONDEMNATION.-- Self condemnation will do you no good. It will rob you of your confidence, joy and your glorious future. In the book of John 8 v 1 - 11 a multitude gathered together and wanted to stone to death a woman who they accused of committing adultery. And when they came to Jesus to seek approval, Jesus told them that whoever was without sin should cast the first stone. No one could do this, therefore if no one could cast the first stone, why should you live in misery by trying to stone yourself with your own hands. Friends any time you engage in self condemnation, you are indirectly picking up a stone and to stone yourself.

There is therefore, no condemnation for those who are in Christ Jesus.

Rom 8 v 1.

Jesus died to set you free and self condemnation does not show the righteousness of God.

(3). AVOID WALLOWING IN SELF PITY.--Self pity does not help and it will literally do you no good because it will draw you into an enclosed state of depression, gloominess, rejection, lower self esteem and defeat. Stop feeling sorry for yourself and look ahead into the future. The future is always bright because with the rising of the sun each day comes new opportunities.

Friends holding onto the past is an act that reflects a state of despair, hopelessness, depression, joy killer and what have you. The Israelite never got to the promised land un time, because although they had left Egypt physically, their hearts and minds was still in Egypt. They refused to forget about their past life in Egypt, they refused to leave Egypt behind, and in their hearts they clung to Egypt.

Sadly because they dwelt too much on their past life in Egypt, anytime they faced the slightest difficulty they would think of going back to Egypt. When they eventually got to the promised land, they carried on with their old lifestyle in Egypt right in the promised land.

If you do not deal or separate yourself from the past it would haunt you and eventually destroy you. Eventually after a long time they ended up going to Egypt. Hence if you dwell too much on your past, it will not only haunt you, but it will eventually swallow you up [backsliding].

Please bear in mind, you can't do anything about your past, and no amount of guilt can change the past, but you can do a lot about your future. If you need healing, Jesus is the balm in Gilead and he alone can help you to overcome the past and you can not do it by yourself. To be successful you must not dwell or brood over the past. Apostle Paul although he did not see Jesus physically as the other 12 disciples, yet he become the top disciple and God wrote 2/3 of the new testament through him. The most important factor that contributed to his success was that he never dwelt on the ugliness of his past life.

Also never ever think it is too late to turn anything around or to serve God. --In the kingdom of God it is never too late to make things right. It is never too late to make that apology to your boss, cousin whoever. Never too late to make a U turn.

Look at the story of Naomi in a strange land, the land of the Moabites. She was surrounded with losses (loss of husband and two sons) and failure. However despite it all, she made a u turn to go back to the land of her birth (Bethlehem), back to the God of Israel.

A U-turn that triggered her to be the channel through which the curse placed on the Moabites by God was removed. Also God used her as an instrument through which the lineage of Jesus can be traced from. She sought a home for Ruth her daughter in law who became the grandmother of David and Jesus is referred to as the root of David.

Also the prodigal son, made a u turn. It does not matter how far the damage, make a u turn today.

KEY NOTE.
THOUGH NO ONE CAN GO BACK AND MAKE A BRAND NEW START, ANYONE CAN START FROM NOW AND MAKE A BRAND NEW ENDING.

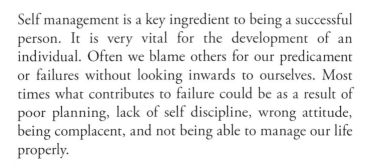

(13)

THE LAW OF SELF MANAGEMENT.

If for any reason you use your tongue to wipe your plate, you have no iota of self control. Eat with a knife to your throat always.

Enoch Adeboye.

Self management is a key ingredient to being a successful person. It is very vital for the development of an individual. Often we blame others for our predicament or failures without looking inwards to ourselves. Most times what contributes to failure could be as a result of poor planning, lack of self discipline, wrong attitude, being complacent, and not being able to manage our life properly.

Self management implies that we bring some amount of discipline into our lives.

Also self management inculcates qualities such as punctuality, discipline, right attitude, subservience, both at work and in our dealings with the public.

Self management helps to control your emotions and keep negative emotions at bay and develop good relationship with people.

Also it makes you to take responsibility for your actions.

Below are five areas to concentrate on in order to keep in step with self management.

a) **DISCIPLINE.**

Self management inculcates discipline. Discipline is very vital to success.

Beloved if you really want to and desire to succeed in life, you have no choice than to submit to discipline. A life without discipline will be very chaotic and there is no way such a life will experience success. Discipline will make you invest, rather than spend money, discipline will make you set goals, discipline will keep you awake while others are sleeping, discipline will make you achieve more, discipline will keep you on track and keep you on your toes.

For every disciplined effort there is a multiple reward.
- Jim Robin.

Discipline is the bridge between goals and accomplishment.
Jim Robin.

Without discipline you are bound to fail. No matter how wealthy you are or how powerful and influential you are, if you lack discipline you are going nowhere to happen.

You would be like a car driven without the necessary brakes. It would just end up in a head long collision. Please and please, submit your life to discipline.

Check the records, there has never been an undisciplined person who was a champion. Regardless of the field of endeavour you will find this to be true.

- Zig Ziglar.

Without discipline, you would be unruly, and an undisciplined life can be likened to a horse driven without bridle in its mouth, it would just run wild.

Have you ever seen a horse run wild? Oh no, it really gets out of control. You need to be disciplined in the area of food, time, sleep, social life and everything. You need to have control over your appetite, your body, your association. etc. You can't say because you have excess money you begin to indulge in mind blowing substances such as cocaine, heroin. Etc. That is going on the path of total destruction.

You can't say because you are in charge of audit, and you start changing figures, that is stealing.

Also you can't say because you have free access to the internet, therefore you can watch pornography.

Also you can't give the excuse that you live in a cold country, so you need to take alcohol and smoke cigarettes to keep warm. They are several ways to keep warm.

Also you can't say because you want to get married, you would sleep with any man that comes your way. You need discipline. You have to learn to say no, when others are saying yes. Be different. Keep your body.

It takes discipline to wake up early at a certain time to worship God.
It takes discipline to keep your mouth shut and stay away from gossip.
It takes discipline not to always try to defend yourself.
It takes discipline to be calm when people expect you to react negatively.
It takes discipline to avoid procrastination.
It takes discipline to put your body, MR FLESH in check.
It takes discipline to be a good listener.
It takes discipline to be in charge of millions of money and not steal.
It takes discipline to wait on God for a spouse, especially when as a man or woman you are not getting younger.

Life itself consist of a lot of areas where you have to apply discipline. However highly anointed you are, if you are not disciplined you are bound to fail. If you are disciplined, the devil would not mess around with you. The devil could not mess around with Elisha, he tried to distract Elisha from getting the double portion anointing by trying to engage him to gossip with the Sons of the prophet. Guess what Elisha was too disciplined and too smart he remained focused. However, Gehazi, Elisha's servant that could have received triple, or even quadruplets portion of Elisha's anointing, lost out due to lack of discipline. Friends submit your life to discipline and the devil will not be able to muck about with you. Samson was highly anointed, but his Achilles hill was immorality and the devil capitalised on this and eventually he was defeated.

Also King Solomon lacked discipline when it came to falling in love and he loved foreign strange women whom God had commanded the Israelites not to associate themselves with nor to to intermarry with them and this great man of God who was so endowed with wisdom and splendour ended up as an idol worshipper.

Discipline paves the way for success and acts as a catalyst that enables you to live the life of your dreams.

Jemima Alara.

b) **HABITS**

Also proper self management will keep you on your toes, you will be able to break bad habits and form good habits.

What are habits. Habits can be defined as a recurrent, often unconscious pattern of behaviour that is acquired through frequent repetition. We have positive and negative habits. Old habits are hard to break because behavourial patterns we repeat are imprinted in our neural pathways, and new habits are hard to form, however it could be done through habitual repetition. Please note that habit formation is slow. Be determined today to break of bad habits and form good habits going forward.

We become what we repeatedly do.

Sean Covey.

How to form new good habits.

Habit formation is a process by which a behaviour through regular repetition becomes automatic or habitual. Habit forming can be analysed in 3 parts,

The cue- The cue is the thing that causes your habit to come about, the trigger to your habitual behaviour. This could be anything that your mind associates with that habit and you will automatically get a habit come to the surface.

The behaviour - The behaviour is the actual habit that you are exhibiting.

The reward.- The satisfaction you derive from that habit.

So from the above we see a loop. An example is,

T.V Program (**Cue),**

Go to the fridge (**Routine)**

Eat a snack (**Reward).**

Also to form good habits have a goal in sight. For instance if you have a goal of loosing weight you will form the habit of eating right, exercising a lot, drinking lots of water etc. Goals guide habits by providing the initial outcome, the motivation for response repetition.

Also if you don't poor water on plants, they will slowly wither and die. Our bad habits will slowly wither and die if we don't give it opportunity to manifest. Don't fight to stop a bad habit, just don't give it opportunity to repeat itself. To overcome a bad habit, develop a new habit.

c) **LAZZINESS.**

Proper self management will also keep you from being lazy. Laziness is an act of pure indiscipline.
'Lazy hands make a man poor, but diligent hands bring wealth'. Proverbs 10 v 4.
Laziness is not good for anyone, laziness is bad. The word of God says in Amos 6 v 1 that

'Woe to you, who is complacent in Zion'.

God is against laziness, God does not work with lazy people. There is so much to do for the kingdom of God and yourself. Lazziness can't produce success. A lazy person will not get up and do anything.

Laziness breeds slothfulness and slothfulness gives birth to complacency. While Jesus was here on earth, he worked from dawn to dusk, going from town to town, from village to village preaching the good news, healing the sick, teaching in the synagogues, grooming the disciples and he always went to the mountains to pray at night. There was no room for laziness in the diary of Jesus, therefore no child of God is permitted to be lazy.

d) **GENERAL WELL BEING.**

Dear friend, I pray that you may enjoy good health and that all may go well with you, even as your soul is getting along well.

3 John v 2.

God wants you to enjoy all round success, both in your well being, your spirit man, and your soul.

Also proper self management will also ensure you keep in step with your general well being. This is very important, because to enjoy your success you need to maintain a healthy and balanced lifestyle. You need to eat healthy and avoid junk food and foods that are not beneficial. You need to take plenty of water. Cut off the sugary frizzy drink, it will do you no good. Take lots of vegetables and fruits. You need to apply a lot of wisdom and eat healthy foods. Also engage in active exercises. Overall ensure you stay healthy and do not take anything for granted.

e) **INTEGRITY**

Integrity is doing the right thing even if no one is watching.
Jim Stovall.

Integrity is maintaining a clear conscience at all times.
Jemima Alara.

Proper self management is for you to maintain and keep your integrity. You can't buy integrity, you earn it. People should be able to trust you. In life trust is at the center of everything. Therefore strive to build your reputation and endeavour to maintain your integrity always.

Honesty is the best policy.
Benjamin Franklin.

Also proper self management would help you manage your success, fame and wealth. It is one thing to be successful and it is entirely another thing to maintain your success and be level headed at all times, We have tales of those who rose to stardom and success but because they lacked self management, they crashed woefully.

They had a very sad and painful ending and their ending was worse than their beginning. Permit me with sadness to name but a few, Elvis Priestly, Micheal Jackson, Whitney Houston all of blessed memory.

Learn to keep in step with good self management, manage yourself properly and watch every sphere of your life turning around for good.

(14)

TAME YOUR TONGUE.

"He who guards his lips, guards his life, but he who speaks rashly will come to ruin."

Proverbs 13 v 3.

In James 3 v 6 explains the tongue as a small part of the body, which if not bridled can corrupt the whole person and sets the whole course of a person's life on fire. We have to watch our tongue.

Two undeniable foundation of success is first of all your mindset and your tongue. Your tongue produces your words and your words shape up the course of your life / destiny. The book of James 3 v 4 describes the tongue as a small rudder which navigates a big ship. Your life is like a ship, your mind is the engine, and your tongue as little as it is, and as insignificant as it looks will actually direct the course of your life. your utterances are powerful, therefore you have to learn how to tame your tongue, otherwise no matter how colorful a destiny you have it can be ruined by the utterances that proceeds out of that tiny rudder called the tongue. The tougue utters what stems from the mind, thus if your mindset is right you will automatically speak right words, words of victory, words of success. With the right words you become unstoppable. However if your mindset is wrong and you keep speaking defeat, failure, tragedy, negative words, so will it be for you. Because you shall have whatsoever you say.

There is an adage which says," You can recover from a slip of foot, but you can hardly recover from a slip of tongue."

Words are very powerful and they carry weight, you have to watch your words, mind how you speak. Your words can either make you or break you. Do not utter words you do not mean. Think carefully before you speak because Proverbs 12 v 18 says "Reckless words pierce like sword."

The word of God admonishes us to always be quick to hear and slow to speak. Your words would either make you or break you. Nobody would hold you to account for being silence, but you would be held to account for what you say. Interestingly this principle is also applied in the worldly system, when you are arrested the first thing the police officer would tell you is that, "you have the right to remain silence and anything you say would be given as evidence against you." Imagine if worldly people know the essence of keeping silence, how much more children of God.

"Even a fool is considered wise when he remains silent."
Proverbs 17 v 28.

James 3 v 2 says "We all stumble in many ways, if anyone is never at fault in what he says, he is a perfect man, able to keep his whole body in check."

1ˢᵗ Peter 3 v 10. "For whoever would love life and see good days must keep his tongue from evil and his lips from deceitful speech."

"When words are many sin is not absent, but he who holds his tongue is wise." Proverbs 10 v 19.

Hence we must strive to tame our tongue so as to either speak the right words or to keep them shut.

Wise men are not always silent, but they know when to be silent.
W. Kumuyi.

In the midst of adversity, just shut up, because you shall have whatsoever you say. When the angel told Zechariah about the birth of John the Baptist, in the first chapter of the book of Luke, he doubted it. After all, he was a priest and he saw an angel, why should he doubt. He did not shut up and keep his doubts to himself, but he spoke up asking, how shall this be, and the angel struck him with dumbness because he did not believe. I am sure if he had shut up, that would not have happened. Meanwhile when the angel visited Mary a young virgin who was not priest, she believed at once and never doubted.

Strive to tame your tongue, use words with restraint because "A man of knowledge uses words with restraint."
Proverbs 17 v 17.

(15)

STAY FOCUSED AND AVOID

DISTRACTIONS.

"You would guard him and keep in perfect and constant peace whose mind is stayed on you, because he commits himself to you, leans on you, and hopes confidently in you." Amp.

Isaiah 26 v 3.

You have to learn the art of staying focused and avoid distractions. There are a lot of things that would seek your attention, and if you focus on the wrong things you would lose track and veer into the wrong direction. Do not give in and try as hard as you can to remain focused all the time. Always keep your mind stayed on God. In all you do, is it business, career, marriage, relationship, etc, always set your focus on Jesus, he is the author and finisher of your faith, keep your eyes on him and you would never fail.

A clear example was Elisha he had served Elijah faithfully and it was time for him to receive the double portion anointing of Elijah. Then came the distractors in the form of the sons of the prophet. Their aim was to distract Elisha by engaging him in gossip. Elisha shunned them immediately, he remained focused and he got the double portion anointing.

Also there were two sisters, called Martha and Mary. Both of them knew Jesus, Jesus was their friend. However Martha was concerned and distracted about other things, while Mary was focused, her attention was for Jesus.

"As Jesus and his disciples were on their way, he came to a village where a woman named Martha opened her home to him. She had a sister called Mary who sat at the Lord's feet listening to what he said. But Martha was distracted by all the preparations that had to be made.

She came to Jesus and asked Lord don't you care that my sister has left me to do the work by myself. Tell her to help me. Martha, Martha, the Lord answered, you are worried and upset about many things, but only one thing is needed. Mary has chosen what is better, and it would not be taken away from her."

Luke 10 v 38 – 42.

If you listen to people or follow the crowd, you are bound to lose focus. King Saul' s problem was that he was always concerned about people's opinion of him and this always swayed his actions and made him to lose focus, from God. He became distracted and focused his attention on redeeming his image, rather than pleasing

God. Imagine acting on songs by a group of women who sang in David's favour, this drove him to jealousy and in a bid to kill David he ended up killing so many prophets of God in a very gruesome and evil manner.

Obstacles are those frightful things you see, when you take your eyes of the goal.

Hanna More.

(16)

AVOID ANGER.

"A fool gives full vent to his anger, but a wise man keeps himself under control."

Proverbs 29 v 11.

"Do not be quick in spirit to be angry or vexed, for anger and vexation resides in the bosom of fools."

Ecclesiastes 7 v 9.

Anger if not properly managed would keep you from your breakthrough. Always be determined to maintain calmness in whatever situation you are going through. Being angry at people or at situations doesn't bring any solution, it rather worsens issues. Also when you are angry at people you become vulnerable to sin and you say and act in ways that are offensive without even being aware of it. However the person on the receiving side may think you are fully aware of what you are doing and would hold you fully accountable for your actions. That is why the word of God in Proverbs 14 v 17 "A quick tempered man does foolish things."

So it is great wisdom, to keep oneself under control. Anger is not a fruit of the Spirit and it stems from the works of the flesh. The works of the flesh which are immorality, impurity, indecency, idolatry, sorcery, enmity, strife, jealousy, represents the old man, the carnal nature. So anytime we want to get angry we should remember that we would be glorifying the carnal man and make him more alive in us.

"Those who belong to Christ Jesus have crucified the sinful nature with its passions and desires." Galatians 5 v 24.

Therefore since you know who you belong to you should endeavour to crucify the flesh and make the fruits of the spirit alive in you, which is Love, joy, peace, patience, kindness, goodness, faithfulness, gentleness and self - control.

The three most harmful negative emotions are anger, guilt and fear. And anger is number one. It is also the strongest and most dangerous of all passions.

Joyce Meyer.

(17)

ALWAYS MAINTAIN A GOOD
DISPOSTION ALL THE TIME.

"He who has no rule over his own spirit is like a city that is broken down and without walls."

Proverbs 25 v 28.

Disposition is how you react to situations. When you face challenges, do you react carnally or do you react based on faith. The word of God says the just shall live by faith. Hence approach all situations with faith. For we walk not by sight, but by faith. Never you always have a disposition of head knowledge.

When Peter walked on sea, his disposition was based on faith, but the moment he began to use his head knowledge, he began to sink.

Friends in life the storms would blow, the wind of adversity would come, unfair weather would rock your boat, but it is your disposition in it all that would determine your victory.

Lots of water surrounding the ship, can't sink the ship, but it is the water that gets into the ship that sinks the ship, hence your disposition would determine if the ocean water would get into your ship or not. Be firm and hold on tight to God. God would never leave you nor forsake you. God is too faithful to fail, too dependable to fail you. He is your ever present help in trouble, not ever past, but ever present. That means he is always present. Your walls are continually before him. Always remember Isaiah 49 v 14-16.

Now a classical example of positive disposition was Hannah in 1st Samuel 1 v 1 - 20. Year in year out Hannah faced the same trouble of taunting from Penninah. And year in year out she reacted with the same negative disposition, by moaning, weeping grieving and being so sorrowful that she would not eat any food. But one day something happened after the usual taunting, she decided to change her disposition into positiveness and she reacted differently.

This time Hannah rose up in faith and went straight before God and poured out her heart to God. She engaged God in a conversation and because she had so much faith that God was not only present with her but was also interested in what she was saying, she committed God by making a vow to Him, to serve as a memorial of the awesome and unique conversation between them.

And she made a vow saying, O Lord Almighty, if you will look upon your servant's misery and remember me and not forget your servant but give her a son, then i will give him to the Lord for all the days of his life.

1st Samuel 1 v 11.

After this episode, Hannah was so confident that the deal was done so;

"She went her way and ate something and her face was no longer downcast." 1st Samuel v 18.

She put on a disposition of cheerfulness, ate her food joyfully and was happy. And this is what followed;

"Early the next morning they arose and worshipped before the Lord and then went back to their home at Ramah. Elkanah lay with Hannah his wife, and the Lord remembered her. So in the course of time Hannah conceived and gave birth to a son. She named him Samuel, saying because I asked the Lord for him." 1st Samuel 1 v 19 -20.

So we see from the above story that having a good disposition goes a long way and it will position you for miracles and favour from God.

Therefore in good or bad situations, let your disposition always be positive.

Further more the secret to maintaining a good disposition at all times is to,
Maintain a heart of gratitude at all times.
Friends at all times, be grateful to God, appreciate God and be thankful to him. Trust me, if not for anything at all, be grateful for the gift of life. Billions of people go to bed each night, thousands never wake up, every minute, every second someone somewhere is dying, but you and

your loved ones are excluded. Whoa, what a priviledge to be among the living.

Therefore you are without excuse. Also don't wait to get your miracle before you thank God. In Christendom, we thank God first before the miracle arrives. The more you thank God and appreciate him, the more God will continue to bless you.

Take for instance this scenario, where you have 5 children and among all of them only one is always grateful and is always thanking you, for everything, both small and big, your guess is as good as mine.

When Jesus healed the ten lepers only one came back to say thank you to Jesus and Jesus perfected his healing, but Jesus also asked 'WHERE ARE THE REMAINING NINE.'

God is still asking that question today, where are the remaining people who will come and say thank you to God. Therefore always maintain an attitude of thankfulness. You know what, the moment you are not thankful you are silently murmuring. You might not know it, but that is the truth. Nature abhors vacuum, so rise up today and fill your hearts with thankfulness, praises etc.

Paul and Silas were imprisoned, they did not let that bother them, and they maintained a good disposition by singing praises to God and God sent his angel to set them free. Amen.

(18)

ALAWYS BE KINGDOM MINDED
AND KINGDOM READY.

"Be dressed ready for service and keep your lamps burning, like men waiting for their master to return from a wedding banquet, so that when he comes and knocks they can immediately open the door for him. You also must be ready, because the Son of Man will come at an hour when you do not expect him."

Luke 12 v 35, 40.

This must always be on your finger tips. By so doing you would always be on your toes. Always note that the main essence of your salvation is to make it to heaven above all else. The pinnacle of success in christendom is when you see God face to face. When you stand before the kings of kings and hear him say to you ' well done thou good and faithful servant.' What a joy, what a blessing to hear those precious words. Your eternity is guaranteed and you will reign with Christ forever. Friends that is success. In whatever we do here on earth we must always bear it at the back of our minds that we are only here temporarily and one day we would go home. This world is not our home.

Every day we live, we take a step towards the grave whether we like it or not. Death is a reality and must come at some point. No one has a choice over death, but everyone has a choice where to spend eternity. Eternity is forever and ever, and there are only two destination where one can spend it, Heaven or hell. The choice is yours.

As children of God we must always be ready for the 2nd coming of our Lord Jesus Christ, it is either this or we translate (die) and go and see him in heaven.
Thus either each way we must be ready. We must always be prepared to meet our maker.

Also being kingdom minded is of so much benefit, it will keep you on your toes and would make you stay away from sin because,

"A little folly, a little sin, causes the oil of apothecary to bring forth a bad smell." Ecclesiastes 1O V 3.

You would also always strive to maintain holiness, because without holiness, no man shall see God.

(19)

THE LAW OF MONEY.

7 LAWS OF MONEY.

1) THE 1ST LAW OF MONEY IS TO HAVE A SOURCE OF INCOME.

'He who does not work will not eat.'
2nd Thess 2 v 10.

Money does not grow on trees, and the fact that you are Christian does not mean that God would rain down money physically from heaven unto your laps. You have to get up and do something and then God would bless the work of your hands by prospering you. You could be self employed, or be in employment, or into business. The whole idea is that you are working. You do the work, no matter how little and God does the prospering. God instructed Isaac to work on the farm and sow in the land in the midst of severe famine and God prospered him, so much that all the people of the land including their king envied him.

In the book of Genesis 2 v 8-9, 15. Although, Adam was surrounded with a vast amount of food, resources, power and authority, yet God commanded Adam to work.

"Now the Lord God had planted a garden in the east, in the Eden and there he put man he had formed. And the Lord God made all kinds of trees grow out of the ground, trees that were pleasing to the eye and good for food.

The Lord God took the man and put him in the garden of Eden to WORK IT AND TAKE CARE OF IT."

God wants everyone to work. God does not encourage laziness, or a something for nothing attitude. God is a God of principles and he laid down the rules, something for something. God gave us Jesus, to get something and that is to reconcile us back to himself. Amen.

Also Apostle Paul despite his heavy schedule and great anointing, he still worked with his hands as a tentmaker to provide a source of income for himself and others.

This is what he had to say in Acts 20 v 33 - 35,

"I have not coveted anyone's silver or gold or clothing. You yourselves know that these hands of mine have supplied my own needs and the needs of my companions. In everything I did, I showed you that by this kind of hard work we must help the weak."

Also he goes on further to say in 1ˢᵗ Thessalonians 4 v 11 – 12 that;

"Make it your ambition to lead a quiet life, to mind your own business and to WORK WITH YOUR HANDS, just as we told you, so that you will not be dependent on anyone."

2) THE 2ND LAW OF MONEY IS YOU ARE NOT TO LOVE MONEY.

"The love of money is the root of all kinds of evil. Some people eager for money, have wandered from the faith and pierced themselves with many grief's."
1st Timothy 6 v 10.

Whoever loves money never has money enough, whoever loves wealth is never satisfied with his income.
Eccles 5 v 10.

Do not love money or the things money can get for you. Do not attach so much love to money. Money is good, but it is of this world and the love of this world is enmity with God. Although money could be a form of defence and provide some sort of security and comfort, we sin when we make it into some sort idol and when we fall in love with it.

You would ask how do we make it an idol? Very simple, remember anything we put ahead of God becomes an idol. For instance if you would rather go to work or stay with your business than going to church, the money from the business or the salary has become an idol. This is not good at all. Idolatry is bad. We are to love God with all our heart and soul, nothing more, and nothing else.

Also in order to avoid loving money, we should see money as just a piece of beautified paper, which we give out in exchange for goods and services. That way we would not want to equate or trade a piece of paper with the presence of God.

Also we have to learn to be content,

"For godliness with contentment is great gain."
1st Timothy v 6-7.

For we brought nothing into this world and we would take nothing out of it.

3) THE 3RD LAW OF MONEY IS THAT DO NOT PAY TOO MUCH ATTENTION TO IT.

'Where your treasure is there your heart will be.'
Matthew 6 v 21.

See money as just an ordinary piece of paper, a legal tender which you give in exchange for goods and services and do not pay too much attention to it.

You can't serve two masters, the god of mammon and God.

"No servant can serve two masters. Either he will hate the one and love the other, or he will be devoted to the one and despise the other. You can't serve both God and money."
Luke 16 v 13.

You are not to serve money, rather put your money to work so that it can serve you.

Let money be your slave and not make yourself a slave to money. Make good bargains, save your money and let it work for you.
John Rockefeller.

You indirectly serve money when you pay too much attention to it and attach so much importance to it.

Also we should not regard money so preciously, nor should we see money as a treasure because,

Where your treasure is there your heart will be. Matthew 6 v 21.

There was a rich young ruler who came to Jesus and asked how he could gain eternal life. Friends to gain eternal life, you must have a heart for God. Jesus asked him about the ten commandments and he replied Jesus that he had obeyed all the 10 commandments right from his youth. However although he was faithful in obeying all the 10 commandments yet his heart, his love, his service, his attention was focused on his wealth and he did not have a heart for God. And Jesus told him what to do so that he would have a heart for God rather than his wealth. Jesus told him to sell all his worldly goods and give to the poor and come and follow him. He bluntly refused and walked away.

What an opportunity, who knows maybe he could have been the thirteenth disciple, but he lost this golden opportunity and chose his money rather than follow Jesus. He walked away sadly. He would rather follow/serve his wealth/money than serve God. We have to take heed. Does our money, job, career, business take priority over our relationship with Jesus? Would we rather miss midweek service just to make more money, or would we open our shops on Sunday morning rather than go to church...etc.

A wise person should have money in their head, but not in their heart.

Jonathan Swift.

4) THE 4TH LAW OF MONEY IS THAT IT MUST BE INCREASED /MULTIPLIED.

"He who gathers money little by little makes it grow."
Proverbs 13 v 11.

God blesses man with wealth, but the power to increase that wealth lies in your hands. God blessed Abraham with wealth, but Abraham increased the wealth. Also God blessed Solomon with wealth, but Solomon increased the wealth. Also Jacob slaved so long for Laban and he had nothing to show for it. However in dream God gave Jacob a vision on how to become rich. Jacob did as told but he did not rest on his oars he increased the wealth by being tenacious, hardworking and always thinking out of the box.

John Rockefeller the worlds richest man, knew the value of money. And when he was asked how he managed to increase his wealth he replied, *"By saving my pennies."*

Do not save what is left after spending, but spend what is left after saving.

Warren Buffet.

There are various ways to increase your wealth and the major way is by investment. Investment is an activity that is done today, but which yields profit at a later date. Investment involves postponing your consumption today in order to put your savings to work. Investment can also be described as the bridge between having savings/surplus cash and reaping returns. In other words, investment has the potential to move the savings surplus funds of one person lending to another who needs or requires those funds. Investment helps you to plan and realize your dream of buying a car, a house etc. Investment puts your money to work and makes your money work for you.

This principle of investment originally started from the bible in Matthew 25 v 14.

To one he gave the five talents of money, to another two talents, and to another one talent, each according to his ability. Then he went on his journey. The man who had received the five talents went at once and put his money to work and gained five more. So also the one with the two talents gained two more.

But the one who had received the one talent went off, dug a hole in the ground and hid his masters money.

After a long time the master of those servants returned and settled accounts with them. The man who had received the five talents brought the other five.

The man with two talents said, see i have gained two more, his master replied, well done, good and faithful servants, come and share in your masters happiness.

Then the man with the one talent said, i was afraid and went out and hid your talent in the ground.

His master replied you wicked servant. You should have my money on deposit with the bankers, so that when i return i would have it back with interest.

The principles learnt here are,

1. God expects money to be multiplied.

Therefore always think of ways to multiply your money, no matter how little it is. It is not how much you earn that matters, it is what you do with how much is in your hands that matters. See money as a seed, which must be planted and allow it to grow, when it grows you can afford to eat the fruits and you will still have your seed in the ground. But if you don't plant and you keep eating your seed, in no time you will run into trouble. No successful wealthy person ever made money without planting their seed of money. **It is the extent of harvest your seed provides that determines your wealth.** Always think of ways to plant your seed. God expects more from the body of Christ, we have left it too long for the unbelievers, it is now time for the body of Christ to arise and everyone should be on their feet and think out of the box and start multiplying your money to bring in the flow of wealth.

2. God maintains accountability.

Friends you have to be trift when it comes to money. Do not spend carelessly, avoid impulse buying. Discipline yourself and engage in strict accountability. The master in the above story represents Jesus, and he held the 3 servants in strict accountability.

3. God wants you to have an investor's mindset.

God was upset with the man who buried the money, because of his negative mindset. He was very narrow minded. A narrow minded person can't go far in life because their thinking is and always will be limited. However Investors are broad minded, they can take on board many things and their thinking is very broad and wide. **Investors always act in faith.** They are always willing to take risk, because they are so positive about their action and this positivity can be referred to as faith.

Jesus commended the two servants, because they had an investors mindset, they thought of ways to multiply the money given to them, while the 3rd servant was sharply rebuked. He was rebuked because of his complacent approach towards what was given to him, he was not ready to think out of the box. God dislikes complacency.

You secure the future when you invest and you can retire comfortably if Jesus tarries.

Also an investor is anyone who decides to put part of his/ her funds in an investment for future benefit. For instance Mary who has decided to use 10% of her monthly salary to buy shares can be described as an investor. If Mary continues at this, in no time she would be financially independent.

Investment is one of the pathway to wealth creation. If you invest your money wisely you can get to wherever you want to go quickly.

Investment is laying out money now, to get more back in the future.

Warren Buffet.

You have to view money as a teammate that you work together with. Always put your money to work and create multiple streams of income. Never have one source of income.

FOR MORE EXPOSITORY FACTS ABOUT MONEY AND WEALTH CREATION I WOULD SUGGEST YOU READ MY BOOK TITLED **THE LANGUAGE OF SUCCESS.**

Be wise, God gives you the power to get wealth, but it is your responsibility to increase your wealth.

5) THE 5TH LAW OF MONEY IS THAT GOD IS THE OWNER OF WEALTH.

God is the owner of wealth. The silver is mine, the gold is mine.

Haggai 2 v 8.

We have to bear this in mind, and must acknowledge that wealth belongs to God. Yes, God is the owner of the heavens and the earth. The earth is the Lords and the fullness thereof. (Ps 24 v 1) The gold, diamond, crude oil and all the mineral resources under the earth and sea belongs to God Almighty.

Child of God, if you want to be rich seek the face God. Seek ye first the kingdom of God and his righteousness and every other thing shall be added unto you. (Matthew 6 v 33).

Is it money spinning ideas you need? Seek God.

Is it the wealth of the gentiles you need? Seek God. Remember the wealth of the gentiles is laid up for the righteous.

Is it the wealth of nations you need? Seek God. Remember nations were bringing gold, timber etc to Solomon every year.

Is it the wealth under the earth and the sea you need? Seek God.

The wealth on the seas will be brought to you.

Isaiah 60 v 5c.

Friends with regard to the wealth of the seas, i will like to share this testimony with you. The richest black woman on planet earth is a woman called Mrs Folorusho Alakija from a country called Nigeria in West Africa. This is a woman from humble background with no University degree. She started of as an office secretary and then later as a clothes maker. Along the line the good Lord orchestrated her steps towards the oil industry. And after so much battles she was able to get an oil bloc license to drill oil in the sea. However this same license she got, other companies rejected because they said there was no prospect of finding oil in that bloc. But she held on in faith to God and believed God that there will be oil in the bloc. Also being a sole entrepreneur she needed to partner with larger companies who had the expertise and equipment to drill for oil.

It was a very challenging time, because every company turned her down. However she held onto God, she prayed and fasted and she entered into a covenant with God. Not too long after that a breakthrough came and a company showed up. The rest is history.

Today that oil bloc that was rejected by everyone has proved to be the most lucrative oil bloc in the history of the world. Thus the the scripture Isaiah 60 v 5c, which says the wealth of the seas will be brought to you, was actually fulfilled in the life of this woman who chose to believe God against all odds and today it has made her the richest black woman on planet earth.

God will do the same for you as well, because God is no respecter of persons. What he did for A, he can do for B. Everything we own or think we have belongs to God and he is the only way to wealth, also he gives us the power and ability to get wealth. Without God we are nothing.

6) THE 6TH LAW OF MONEY IS THAT YOU ARE NOT PERMITTED TO BORROW.

Do not borrow. *"Thou shall lend to many nations, and you shall not borrow."*

Deut 28 v 12c

The word of God admonishes us not to borrow because the borrower is a servant to the lender. Jesus became poor that we might be rich. You are rich why should you borrow. Jesus redeemed us in order that the blessings given to Abraham might come to the Gentiles through Christ Jesus. Galatians 3 v 14.

From the above we have been given the catalyst for wealth, therefore as a child of God you are not supposed to be poor, neither are you permitted to borrow. Abraham always gave. Jesus also gave, he was in absolute control of wealth. Jesus has the key to wealth, and in Matthew 17 v 27 he put money, a gold coin in the mouth of a fish. What a great God we serve.

7) THE 7TH LAW OF MONEY IS WE ARE TO HONOUR GOD WITH OUR MONEY.

Honour the Lord with thy tithes and offerings.

We honour God with our money, by tithing and offering. We have to give God 10% our income. When we tithe we are putting God first, ahead of everything. We are saying God I honour you and i love you and i am putting you first before my money. This money can't take your place in my life. Tithing and offering keeps us in check, and makes us to always remember that God is in charge and he would always take the center stage in our finances.

Never put God behind, put God first by tithing.

Time is money and everyday we wake up we are presented with a free 24 hour currency. Learn to tithe 10% of this free currency which totals to just 2 hours, 40 minutes to God and watch your life turn around for good.

Jemima Alara.

Also when we tithe, our wealth is insured with the best insurance company that ever existed. John D. Rockefeller, one of the wealthiest men the world has ever seen was taught at a very early age on tithing by his mother and he followed his mother's instruction's to the latter. He started tithing from the tender age of 16. Today even in death he is worth 340 billion US dollars and his wealth is still increasing. His record is yet to be beaten. If you honour God, God would honour you.

(20)

THE LAW OF DUPLICATION.

To be successful in any area of life, it is good to study the lives of others who had succeeded in that particular area, to find out what they did which other people ignored.

Enoch Adeboye.

The surest way of success is to model someone who has already done what you want or has achieved success in the particular field you desire. One key note about success is that it leaves clues. Also all results are produced by some specific set of actions. Every cause results in an effect. For every effect to happen there is an action / cause you must take. If you exactly reproduce some ones actions, then you can produce the same results.

Duplication is all about modelling after what someone else has done. You study successful people to discover the actions they took to produce the results they got, then you duplicate that particular action they took and you would get the same results in much less time.

Duplication saves you time. What took a successful person a longer period of time including lots of trial and error, you can step in, model the persons actions and in a matter of moments, months or at least in a lot less time than it took the person whose results you desire to duplicate. You can get the same results.

Please note that whatever you desire to be, there are models for it. For instance if you want to be an excellent athelete with the prospect of winning gold medals, all you have do is to model after those who have already achieved that feat. Take the actions they took and you would produce the same results.

If you want the almighty God to refer to you as his friend or as a man after his own heart all you need to do is to study the life of Abraham and model after the actions he took and in no time, God will refer to you as his friend. Similarly study and read everything about King David, model his actions and soon the Almighty God would refer to you as a man / woman after his heart.

Also if you want to be a successful entrepreneur, like Richard Branson, get books and information about him, model after him and in no time you would start producing the results he is producing.
If you want to be a successful filmmaker, read all you can read about Steven Spielberg, do what he did and you would produce the same results he is producing.

Also note one good thing about successful people is that they never hoard information, they are all too excited to share their success stories and they do this at every opportunity they get. The problem is that majority of people are too ignorant or they are too busy to read books written by these successful people or they are busy trying to come up with their own method to succeed. Please don't waste your time anymore, unveil your ignorance and go out there and seek information, read books and endeavour to understudy successful people.

Elisha understudied Elijah, he actually served Elijah and in the end he became a duplicate of Elijah. He even outweighed and did double times of what Elijah did.
Finally those who have discovered this secret of duplication and adopted it, have become the movers and shakers of this world. They are referred to as professional modellers. Steven Spielberg modelled people at the Universal Studios and today he is the most successful film maker the world has ever seen.

That some achieve great success is proof to all that others can achieve it as well.

Abraham Lincoln.

(21)

DEVELOP YOURSELF / ENHANCE

YOUR POTENTIALS.

"If the axe is dull and its edge unsharpened, more strength is needed but skill will bring success.
Ecclesiastes 10 v 10.

Life in general is dynamic and not static. Things change, nothing is ever the same, what was obtainable five years ago, would no longer be obtainable presently. For instance few years back there was nothing like a computer, or Ipad what was available was a typewriter. Now we have computer, laptop and beyond which is tablet and as time goes on there would be new innovations, new ideas, new concepts etc. Hence as children of God we have to be on top, we do not have to remain static, we have to look for areas to improve in our lives. For instance, you can go back to school and get more qualifications, you can acquire more skills, improve your career or even change it, you can learn a new trade, there are so many things you can do to enhance yourself, rather than fold your arms and do nothing.

For instance if you are a teacher, go for further training and strive to be the best in your field. As a barber, tradesman you can improve yourself. Make yourself and your life count.

The secret to success is to do the uncommon things commonly well.

John Rockefeller.

God has deposited a spirit of excellence in you, but it is up to you to walk in it by enhancing the potentials embedded in you.

Also God is committed to bless the work of your hands, what is that work of your hands, that thing that you do that stands you out, that distinguishes you from others.

God has given everyone a talent, you have to discover your niche and work on it. Your success is all for the glory of God and for the edification of the body of Christ.

(22)

BE CONFIDENT IN YOURSELF.

"God has not given us a spirit of fear, but of sound mind."

2nd Tim 1 v 7.

You have to be aware of who you are in Christ Jesus. Take the limits off yourself. Do not place any limitation on yourself, do not say I can't do this, I can't do that.

"You can do all things (not some things) through Christ that strengthens you."

Go through life with this mind set in you. Do not walk with your heads bowed down, do not let challenges dictate your mood and composure, shake it off and move on.

I'm never gonna put boundaries on myself ever again. I am never gonna say I can't do it. I am never gonna say maybe. I'm never gonna say, I don't think I can. I can and I will.
-Nadiya Hussain.

This speech was given by this young lady Nadiya Hussain who won the Great British Bake Off 2015. She beat several contestants to win this competitive award. Her success is very inspiring because, she is from a Bangladesh descent where baking is rare. Also she learn't how to bake casually from high school. However she entered this competition and put all her efforts, took all the limits off and she beat other contestants who have been baking all their lives. Always see yourself as a success and you would be one, there is a deposit in you, there is a fountain of living waters in you, waiting to flow out of you, do not hinder the flow with your lack of confidence. Know who you are in Christ.

You only place limits on yourself, when you don't know who you are in Christ, however the moment you come to the understanding of who you are in Christ you will shake the limits off.

You are the apple of God's eyes, you are a royal generation, Gods own chosen vessel. You are seated on high with Christ Jesus. Beloved you are too much, the seed of greatness is in you. The whole world is waiting for your manifestation, get ready to manifest, arise and shine, rise up as an eagle. There is a glory waiting to be revealed through you.

(23)

DO NOT RUN AWAY FROM CHALLENGES. LEARN TO DEAL WITH YOUR GIANTS.

"If you have raced with men on foot and they have worn you out, how can you compete with horses."
Jeremiah 12 v 5.

It is very important to have this understanding in you and always see every challenge as a stepping stone to your next level in life. Every challenge is a testimony, without the test, there can be no testimony.

In life, challenges would come, the storm would blow, the so called giants would surface, but do not ever think of running away. Where are you running to? Stand and face the storm, face that mountain and speak to that mountain until the mountain gives way for you to go through. When faced with a mountain, don't quit until you climb over it. Running away worsens the problem, it does not solve it. Look at the children of Israel, because of their refusal to go into the promise land and face their giants, they opted to run away from it and return back to Egypt. That decision never solved their problem, it only worsened their condition because,

1. They incurred the wrath of God
2. Also all those people that murmured never got into the promised land/inheritance.
3. They remained stagnant for forty more years, where as this was a journey that was supposed to only take less than 40 days.

This was very unnecessary and avoidable. All they needed to do was to march and confront the giants.

In Zechariah 4 v 7 Zerubbabel was faced with a mountain like situation, and he faced the mountain squarely and spoke prophetically over the mountain.

"Who are thou O mighty mountain before Zerrubabel you will become like a plain ground."

This is how God expects us to deal with our mountain like challenges. Challenges can come in different form, it could be a health challenge, financial, marital, career, family, relationship and all sorts.

David stood and faced the giant Goliath while everyone was running away and that particular act aligned him into his destiny. Remember he had been anointed, but God used that act to put him in the palace where he served before King Saul and also to prepare him for all the battles ahead of him.

Don't analyze the storm, don't even bother to find out where it is coming from, or why it is blowing in your direction, don't even try to run away from it, do what the eagle does, dive right into the storm and use the currents to soar high into your next level in life.

Jemima Alara.

Also when the temple of God was being rebuilt by the Jews, we had Sanballat and Tobiah who tried to frighten the people in order to hinder the work of God, but the Jews refused to be hindered and stood to face the human mountain, they built by day and by night until the walls of Jerusalem was completed.

(24)

DO NOT BE HASTY IN TAKING

DECISIONS

"A simple man believes anything, but a prudent man gives thought to his steps."

Proverbs 14 v 15.

As a golden rule, never take decisions hastily. Remember most of what befalls us are as result of decisions wrongly and hastily taken. If you take a wrong decision, you would pay a heavy price for it and if you take decisions rightly you would reap the benefit. Please do not take decisions when you are upset or in a bad mood.

Always stay calm and hand over everything to God because he knows best, he knows what you don't know, sees what you can't see, hears what you can't hear, he is present where you can not be present, God is awesome and he is Omiprescent.

After you commit it into the hands of God, then think it through carefully as you do the Spirit of God would give you guidance. Weigh the options, look at the pros and cons of the decision before you, does the advantage outweighs the disadvantage and if it does, then go ahead, however if it is the opposite, then have a rethink. Also seek godly counsel for in the multitude of counsel there is safety.

Plans fail for lack of counsel, but with many advisers plans succeed.

(Prov 15 v 22).

(25)

LEARN TO HAVE A RIGHT ATTITUDE

Of all the attitudes we can acquire surely the attitude of gratitude is the most important and by far the most life changing.

Zig Ziglar.

It's not what happens to you that determines how far you will go in life. It is how you handle what happens to you that would determine how far you would go in life. You can't tailor make situations in life, but you can tailor the attitudes to fit those situations before they arise.

How far you go in life, is dependent on your attitude. It is not your Aptitude that would determine your altitude but it is your attitude that will determine your altitude in life. Always maintain a right attitude, no matter what you are going through. In life you would face all sorts of challenges, because the bible did not say IF YOU GO THROUGH THE FIRE, but it says WHEN YOU GO

THROUGH THE FIRE. "IF" is an optional word, but "WHEN" is a sure word, so beloved be prepared because the fire would come, the winds of adversity would blow, the storms would rage, but through it, if you maintain the right attitude you would surely overcome and be more than a conqueror, you would be like Mount Zion which can not be moved. Amen.

Also always maintain the attitude of humility, never look down on anyone. Be humble. Take for instance the story of Naman, he was healed of leprosy through the counsel of a common girl. Your attitude is very crucial to your success as a Christian. Most times people blame the devil, meanwhile they are the architect of their own problems. Look at the classical example of king Saul, he was favoured above all other Israelites and had the honour of being Israel's first king. He could have been one of the finest king Israel ever produced, but he had a wrong attitude and it was this wrong attitude that ruined him. He was disobedient and unrepentant. He had an attitude that was all about, me, myself and I, an attitude of arrogance/pride.

He had no reverence for God in his heart. And when his mistakes where pointed out to him, he was never repentant. So negative was his attitude that, a group of women who sang a song in David's favour, drove him to jealousy and in his desperate bid to kill David he ended up killing many prophets of God in a very gruesome manner. King Saul's attitude grieved God so much that God had to reject him. Friends we need to have the right attitude to please God.

A person with a right attitude would always praise God in all situations, will always be grateful to God, will always be thankful to God and will always be humble. King David always maintained a right attitude, despite all the challenges he faced, he clung unto God, and at the end of the day God referred to David as a man after his own heart.

Also, have the right attitude of building bridges and not burning bridges. You are not an island. You need godly people you can run to and talk to when the chips are down. Build good relationships, invest in others, be nice, bless people, remember their birthdays, interact wisely. We have the good, bad and ugly. Jesus mixed with all sorts and dealt wisely with them. He knew Judas was a thief, yet he did not expel him from being his disciples. But Jesus dealt wisely with his disciples and out of the 12, he had just four of them, that he had special relationship with different from the others. These four can be referred to as the inner circle inside a circle. And Jesus took them with him to the Mount of transfiguration.

So we have to relate, we can't help by not relating, but we have to deal wisely and select our inner circle wisely.

Also maintain the right attitude of not being judgemental about others. Most Christian's are guilty of this and are not even aware of it. You are not to judge anyone, nor condemn anyone and you are not to discriminate as well, by saying this is a muslim, that is an hindu, that is an homosexual, and I would not interact with so and so, x, y, z.

Remember that Jesus died for everyone, both the pagan, muslim, atheist, drug addict, prostitute, thief, and what have you. Jesus shed his blood, and it was not anyone's else blood. Therefore who are we to discriminate and not walk in love.

Also we have to develop a right attitude of refraining from anger.

"Do not be quick in spirit to be angry or vexed, for anger and vexation resides in the bosom of fools." Ecclesiastes 7 v 9.

Anger if not properly managed would keep you from your breakthrough. Always be determined to maintain calmness in whatever situation you are going through. Being angry at people or at situations does not solve any problems, it rather worsens issues. Anger is not a fruit of the Spirit. Anger stems from the works of the flesh

(26)

HAVE A POSITIVE MENTALITY

As a man thinks in his heart, so is he.

You cannot have a positive life and a negative mind.
Joyce Meyer.

The battlefield of life starts in the mind. You need to win the battle of life in your mind, to be able to enjoy success. Both defeat and success starts from your thoughts. Your thoughts would either make you or break you. You have to have a grip over your thoughts, because no matter what you do both the negative and positive thoughts will come. You can't stop the negative thoughts, but you can stop it from taking roots in your life. Don't allow it to settle in your mind. Always stay abreast and keep meditating, keep thinking positive. Your positive thoughts will transform your life to become a bundle of success.

We are what our thoughts have made us, so take care about what you think. Words are secondary. Thoughts live they travel far.

Swan Vivekananda.

Always think positive, never think negative. Guard your thoughts to always be positive minded, no matter what challenges you are going through. In life the storms would blow, trials would come, tough time would show up, impossible situation would stare at you, but in everything, learn to stay positive.

Negative thoughts defeat the purpose of faith and makes you lose hope, when you should be hopeful.

One cannot be prepared for something while secretly believing it will not happen. - Nelson Mandela.

Negative minded people never inherit the promises of God, because they always walk by sight and not by faith. To inherit God's promises you must walk by faith. Most of the Israelites did not enter the promised land due to their disbelief which was as a result of their negative mentality.

"And to whom did God swear that they would never enter his rest if not to those who disobeyed. So we see that they were not able to enter, because of their unbelief." Hebrews 3 v 18 - 19.

Also as a result of their negative thinking, when Jesus the long awaited Messiah showed up, they refused to accept him. Their minds were so encrypted with negativity that despite all the miracles they saw Jesus perform, it did not move them into believing that he was the long awaited Messiah.

As far as they were concerned, they felt nothing good can come out of Nazareth where Jesus was from. How sad. Beloved it is costly to have a negative mentality. Imagine, they beheld the glory of the only begotten Son of God, they saw him, he walked amongst them daily, but due to their negative mind set, they rejected him.

To succeed you need to maintain a positive mindset. Your success is driven by your mindset. It is possibility mentality that makes a giant. You need the mentality of a star so that you don't end up as a failure. You have to tune the thermostat of your brain to stay permanently positive. Always operate from the view point and dynamic sense of possibility. Take this quick test,

1. Do you see things working out for you?

2. Do you expect negative or positive results?

3. Do you always base things on probabilities.

4. Do you entertain fear, obstacles, roadblocks?

5. Do you have a depressed feeling of hopelessness, gloominess, discouragement etc.

6. Do you feel life is unfair?

If your tick for all or some of the above is yes, then it is time to wake up and drop the cloak of negativity and put on the cloak of positiveness.

Please note all successful people have one thing in common and that is they never entertain negativity. Richard Branson a world class entreprenuer is a candidate in the school of possibility, hence he is able to achieve record breaking events. He overcame and climbed every hurdle, obstacle and mountain to be where he is today. He wouldn't be where he is today if he was a candidate of the school of negativity.

Please in all you do, never conform to negativity, always stay positive. You have the mind of Christ and there is no negativity with God, BECAUSE WITH GOD ALL THINGS ARE POSSIBLE. Always stay positive, because your God is always and forever a winner and you are on the winning side.

(27)

ALWAYS BE ON THE MOVE / TAKE A STEP

A journey of a thousand miles always begins with a step.

Lao Tsu.

In life never ever, take the static position, refuse to be at a standstill position no matter the challenges you face. The key to success or one of the languages of success is never to remain static, refuse to be stagnant, keep moving. Do not allow your challenges dictate your pace in life. So many people fail because they fail or refuse to take a step. To overcome you need to keep moving, there is no room for standstill, watching or waiting to see what would happen.

Step out and take a step, it does not matter how tiny the step is, it could be tiny, a step is a step. The hare would step out very swiftly, and a tortoise would also step out slowly, but both of them are taking steps, though they would both arrive at different times, but at least they are heading somewhere. If you remain at one spot, you are heading nowhere, going nowhere to happen. You have got to make it happen, nothing happens by chance or by accident.

Success does not answer to anyone who stands aloof, doing nothing. You have to be up, jerk yourself up and move. God deals with those who are stirred up. In the book of 2nd kings 7 v 3 - 20, tells us the story about four lepers, who refused to allow their circumstances hinder them, and rather than sit down and be static, they decided to keep moving in search of food, and as they were moving God helped them. However in that same city, they were able bodied men, but they all refused to move.

Do you know why if you do not do anything success would not respond to you, because the moment you take a standstill position and fold your arms then automatically you have resigned to fate and before long you start murmuring. God hates murmuring. Get yourself out and do something, it does not matter how little, give a push. Motionless people never succeed. Do you need a job, get up and go out, do you need a career get up and enhance yourself.

According to Martin Luther, he states that in life do not be static, IF YOU CAN NOT FLY, THEN RUN, IF YOU CAN NOT RUN, THEN WALK, IF YOU CAN NOT WALK, THEN CRAWL, BUT BY ALL MEANS KEEP MOVING AND YOU WOULD SURELY GET THERE.

A journey of a thousand miles always begins with a step. Make that move now, take that step, get that form, apply for that job now, build your career now, enrol for that course now. Now is the word.

(28)

DO NOT BE A SPECTATOR

Do not stand with your hands akimbo and watch others take the center stage in life, by the way those in the center stage have only one head, two hands, two legs the same as you have, so whats your excuse?

Jemima Alara.

Get involved. Do not just watch things happen, but make things happen. In life there are 3 set of people, we have the

1. **SPECTATORS** [fans], -- Fans are grouped among the multitude. Spectators watch things happen, they watch people make history. Fans are never reckoned with, they are always grouped together and referred to as and co. All they do is to make so much noise and cheer those who are making things to happen. Spectators are always on the look out for actors. They don't condemn, they enjoy taking the back bench position and watch things happen. They prefer to be onlookers and they never desire to be participants.

You have to decide not to be a fan in life, refuse to be a fan, come out of the crowd, come out of the mixed multitudes and make your life count.

2. **ACTORS** - These are the real players in life. These are people who make things happen. They occupy the center stage. The main arena and people watch them make history. Every child of God is a star, the world is supposed to watch you make things happen. Actors are celebrated and remembered long after they have left this world, because they leave their footprints on the sands of time. While everyone is busy looking into the skies and admiring the stars, actors climb the mountains and grab a star.

Also according to Williams Shakespeare, he states that life is a stage and everyone plays a part. However you can determine the role or part you want to play. You can decide to play the part of a backbencher, or a spectator who enjoys cheering up the actors, or a commentator who are hardcore critics, always criticising the actors, or you can decide to get into the main arena, the center stage and let the world watch you in admiration playing your part.

You can either waltz boldly on to the stage of life and live the way you know your spirit is nudging you to, or you can sit quietly by the wall, receding into the shadows of fear and self doubt.
Oprah Winfrey.

3. **COMMENTATORS** -- These are the critics, all they do is to comment, analyse the actors who make things to happen. Nothing is ever right before them, They must always have something to say. They are going nowhere to happen, they can be classified as a rolling stone that gathers no moss. They go through life unnoticed and refuse to change. They never throw their weight behind the actors, rather their aim is to seek the downfall of the actor.

In the bible the Pharisees were a perfect example of commentators. All they did was to criticise and condemn Jesus who made things happen. They kept commenting about the actor (Jesus), they were always debating amongst themselves on how to bring Jesus down. Eventually they couldn't take it anymore and they plotted a downfall for Jesus. The opposite happened. Rather than a downfall for Jesus, it was a divine elevation. There is no gain in being a commentator.

Think this through, at the end of your life, which category do you want to be known for? Is it as A SPECTATOR, AN ACTOR, OR A COMMENTATOR?

(29)

RECREATE YOUR WORLD WITH

YOUR WORDS

"From the fruit of his lips a man is filled with good things".

Proverbs 12 v 14.

In the beginning God created the world by speaking. God spoke this world into being. Now the devil came to mar what God had created. You do not have to live in a world that is marred by the devil. No, never, as a child of God you have the power to recreate your world. God has deposited in you what it takes to do this and you have to speak the right words. Speak the word of life which is the word of God to recreate your world.

The word of God in Matthew 18 v 18 says, Whatever you decree on earth shall be established in heaven.

You shall decree a thing and it shall come to pass.

Job 22 v 28

Whoa, what a wonder, go ahead,
Do not be silent. Romans 10 v 8 says "The word is near you, it is in your mouth and in your heart"

Speak right words, always positive words. Speak your marriage into fulfilment, speak your way into financial prosperity, speak your career to life, recreate your world.

In Ezekiel 37 there was a valley of dead bones, soldiers who had died and their bones had dried up, a very hopeless situation, but God took Ezekiel to the valley and asked him if the bones could live again. Ezekiel in his heart knew that it was impossible, but he trusted God. God did not tell Ezekiel to weep over the bones, or to meditate over the situation, neither did God tell him to analyse the situation at the valley of dry bones, as some of us are good at analyzing our circumstances.

We would sit down and critically analyse our challenges and would question ourselves, how can God solve this problem for me. Friends, God challenged Ezekiel and told him to swing into action by prophesying, by speaking the word of life, the word of faith unto the dry bones and as Ezekiel spoke, suddenly there was a rattling, there was a noise and the bones came together, and out of the valley of dry bones there arose an exceedingly great army.

Whao! what an awesome God we serve.

With the word of God you can recreate anything, you can call forth those things that be not into life. You can turn your dry lands into a fruitful land, you can turn the hopeless case to be a hopeful case, you can turn that dull child to be a bright child, you can turn that tiny business into a multinational business empire, you can turn that husband that is wife beater into wife lover, friends you can turn just anything around with the word of God.

Do not be silent, open your mouth wide and God will fill it up for you. Friends it is very vital to open your mouth and prophesy. This is a commandment and not a suggestion.

Anytime you speak the word which is the Logos, you activate the Rhema, which is the power in the word. Therefore to see that mountain / that unpleasant situation change in your life you have to speak the word of God over it. Speak and command that mountain to go away. A big mountain was confronting Zerrubabel in Zechariah 4 v 7 and he spoke to the mountain saying who art thou o great mountain before Zerrubabel, you will become a level ground. Therefore rise up and speak to your challenges and watch them turn into success for you.

If you have faith, you SAY to this mountain, go throw yourself into the sea, and it will be done. Nothing will be impossible for you.

Matthew 21 v 21

From now, use your tongue right and begin to speak to any mountain confronting you. There is power in words.

Also understand that words are seeds, which when spoken will germinate and bring forth fruits. Therefore if you keep speaking positiveness, you will automatically reap positiveness and if you keep speaking negativeness, you will automatically reap negativeness. You can call it the law of sowing and reaping. Yes it is, you reap what you sow. Therefore going forward, determine and purpose in your heart to only sow seeds of positiveness so you can reap the fruits of positiveness.

Destiny is calling out to you, destiny is waiting for you. Friends according to Isaiah 60 v 2, it says that darkness hovers over the world, do not allow this darkness to hoover over you, you have the word of life, which is light and the word shines in the darkness. So to shine or be a success in this dark world you need the word of God and when you speak the word of God you activate it and cause light to shine on your path, for the entrance of Gods word brings light. And his word is a lamp unto our feet and a light unto our path.

Also choose your words carefully because words are so powerful, avoid careless speaking. If you continue speaking life you would see life, if you speak death you would see death.

Proverbs 18 v 21 states that "The power of life and death is in the tongue and those who love it will eat its fruit."

If you are not happy with any situation in your life, quietly locate the word of God that addresses that situation and keep speaking that particular word over and over again, until you see a change. God speaking in Jeremiah 23 v 29 says,

"Is my word not like fire and a hammer that breaks the rock into pieces."

Also in Hebrew 4 v 12." The word of God is living and active. Sharper than any double – edged sword"

What more proof do we need.

Prophesy the word of God, prophesy over your circumstances, prophesy over your marriage, prophesy over your children, finances etc.

(30)

THE FAVOUR FACTOR.

"His anger is for a moment, but his favour is for lifetime."

Psalm 30 v 5a.

Favour is an act you do not deserve. It is undeserved kindness of God. Every believer enjoys the favour of God to some extent. The fact that you are saved, shows you that you have the favor of God on you. For by grace we have been saved, not by works lest any man should boast. Grace is unmerited favour. However i am talking about a higher dimension of favour, an extra ordinary favour that everyone would know without a shadow of doubt that it could only be God who made it possible.

It was said of Joseph,' But for God',
It was said about Queen Esther that ' But for God',
It was said about Daniel when he came out alive out of the lion's den that ' But for God'.
It was said to Ruth a Moabite who ended up becoming the great grandmother of Kind David through whom

the lineage and ancestry line of Jesus is traced that 'But for God'.

This is the kind of favour i am talking about. God's favour is in degrees and the extent of degree of favour you enjoy from God is determined by how much you please God.

"For surely O Lord you bless the righteous, you surround them with your favour as with shield." Psalm 5 v 12.

The God we serve is a God of favour. He raises the poor out of the dunghill and makes him to sit with the kings and princes. 1st Samuel 1 v 8.

In the bible we have example of people who enjoyed God's favour, King David was one of them. Right in the fields God's favour located him and brought him out of nowhere and set him high as the king of Israel. Not only so, God was so proud to trace the lineage of Jesus through the ancestry line of King David.

Also among all the virgins in Israel, favour found Mary, and her womb carried our Lord Jesus Christ.

Also favour located Esther and set her as a queen in a foreign land. She was chosen out of multitudes of young maidens. We are told that the contest was in its 3rd year running, when Esther appeared before the King, but the moment the king saw her, he was so pleased with her and without hesitation he set the royal crown on her head, and threw a big bash for her. That means in the first year, the king was not pleased, in the second year he was not pleased, however in the third year, here comes along the Lords chosen, the Lords anointed in the form of Esther and the king was finally pleased. Friends God's timing is always perfect. God is never late, never early, but always on time.

Friends Esther found favour, obviously she was not the most beautiful and fairest but favour found her. In this crazy world, we all need the favour of God. Favour would make us excel in life, favour would make you fly when others are busy walking. Favour would make you soar high.

Favour made Joseph a slave to become the second highest ruler in a strange land.

Favour made Boaz a rich man to locate Ruth an ordinary labourer.

Favour located Daniel and his 3 friends and God lifted them up in a strange land. Daniel a slave, served as a respectable and honourable man with 3 kings consecutively.

All these found favour before God. However, this favour did not just come like that, they activated it. What did they do?

1. They did not COMPROMISE their stand for God. Joseph refused to compromise, despite the carrot of temporary favour and evil pleasure dangling before him. Here was a young man sold into slavery forever without no hope of a future, yet he refused to compromise. He was in a very desperate situation, but he chose to be faithful to God.

Some people would have gone for this and see it as an opportunity for their escape, they would even question God and doubt God as well, but Joseph held on even when he was thrown into the dungeon for many years. And in the end he enjoyed the extraordinary favour of God.

2. They DEDICATED their lives to God and were FAITHFUL to God. Ruth dedicated her life to the God of Israel when she left the land of Moab and clung unto Naomi an old woman with no viable prospects and followed her to the land of Israel. She made up her mind never to return to the land of Moab forever and ever and she told Naomi that the God Naomi served would be her God also and she would serve him.

    That is how God wants us to cling to him. God loves faithfulness and rewards faithfulness as well. Naomi held on despite the distractions, Orpah, her sister in law was a distraction, even at a point her mother in law also posed as a distraction when she urged her to go back, but she persisted. God favoured her and overturned a verdict he had issued against the Moabites. God had said in Deu 23 v 3 that no Moabites shall enter into the assembly of God. But not only did God turn this around, God made Ruth to be the great grandmother of David through whom the lineage of Jesus is traced. Hallelujah, what a great God we serve.

3.   They made SACRIFICES and chose to go Gods way. Moses left all the pleasures of Egypt and preferred to endure suffering with the Israelites.

'He chose to be mistreated along with the people of God rather than to enjoy the pleasures of sin for a short time. He regarded disgrace for the sake of Christ as of greater value than the treasures of Egypt.'

Hebrew 11 v 25 - 26.

4.   They followed INSTRUCTIONS and were willing to be led. God is the great shepherd and he loves to lead his sheep. Not every Christian is ready to be a sheep. Queen Esther in the book of Esther had a sheep like attitude. She was always ready to listen to Mordecai and follow his instructions. You will win Gods favour if you abide by his instructions.

Also even after Esther became queen, she still carried on with her sheep like attitude and she still followed the instructions of her shepherd. (Mordecai) And as a result of this, multitudes of Jewish lives were saved.

5.   David had a HEART FOR GOD. He loved God with all his heart and he served God all the days of his life. He also sought after God always. 'As the dear pants for streams of water, so my soul pants for you o God. Ps 42 v 1.

6. Daniel PURPOSED in his heart to serve God. Daniel 11 v 8.

From the above we can see that all the characters mentioned took a step, they did something that pleased God and made God to move and favour them extraordinarily. They pulled various strings that activated favour for them. Is it Joseph who refused to compromise and will rather risk his life than to sleep with Potiphar's wife, or is it Daniel and his three friends who purposed in their hearts not to defile themselves with the kings food, or is it Ruth who left all and clung unto the God of Israel, or is it Abraham who obeyed the call of God and left his nation entirely at the age of 75, not only that he also obeyed God to the point of offering his son Isaac as a sacrifice to God until God stopped him.

These all took a stand, they all activated favour. What stand are you ready to take or what strings are you ready to pull in order to enjoy extraordinary favour from God. Beloved choose to please God and as you do so God will surely arise and favour you.

THE LAW OF MOTIVATION.

Motivation is that desire within you, that fire that sparks naturally inside of you that gears you to do a particular thing or achieve a specific feat effortlessly.
Jemima Alara.

Motivation is a reason, something within you that drives you on and on to achieve your desired goal. Motivation can be likened to passion. You can't succeed in any field if you do not have motivation or interest in that field. It is motivation that drives the computer scientists through years of dedication to create breakthroughs in that chosen field.

Motivation will make you take sacrifices and make you delay your gratification because you know your priorities. Motivation is powered by desire and ambition. When there is motivation, there is initiative, direction, courage, energy and you automatically build the persistence required to follow your desired goals. Also, motivation is a sign of strong desire, enthusiasm and willingness to do whatever it takes to achieve what one sets out to do.

Motivation becomes strong when you have a vision, a clear mental image of what you want to achieve and also a strong desire to manifest it. In such situation motivation awakens inner strength and power and pushes you forward toward making your vision a reality.

A motivated person takes action and does whatever it needs to achieve his or her goals.

Further more motivation is one of the most important keys to success. When there is a lack of motivation you either get little or zero results, but when there is motivation you attain greater and better results and achievements. For instance a student who lacks motivation to study will not study and a student who is highly motivated would devote many hours to his studies, definitely you can guess the outcome of the results they both will get. A motivated person takes action and does whatever it needs to achieve his or her goals.

When you are motivated or when you are driven with passion you enjoy what you are doing. People rarely succeed unless they have fun in what they are doing. When all else fails it is your passion / motivation that will keep you going.

Please it is very important to note and understand that to find out what your passion in life is, you don't have to look to far, all you need to find out is to locate where your motivation lies. For instance a person whose talent is drawing, will always be motivated naturally towards drawing and artistic works. Such a person can spend hours and hours drawing and will love every inch of it without getting bored. However another person whose talent is not drawing can never and will never be motivated to draw. And if forced to draw will not gladly sit down for even a fraction of an hour. Thus motivation unlocks your passion / talent and your talents will lead you to success. Your talents will make you stand before kings and not mere men.

THE ROAD TO SUCCESS STARTS WITH DISCOVERING YOUR PASSION / YOUR TALENT.

Passion is the secret ingredient. Just being an idea person is not enough to guarantee success, being passionate about what you do, will guarantee success.

Steve Jobs.

Now to find out what your passion is or to know whether you are motivated or not, look inwards and ask yourself the following questions,

1. What do I love doing? Finding out what you love doing is the first key step to directing your passion.

2. What can keep me awake?

3. What do I do effortlessly, that others struggle to do?

4. Discover what you do very well? What are you simply good at.

If you are good at something you have some solid ground to build on. Everyone has a talent or talents, but you will never discover your talent unless you seek out to discover it. Talents can be likened to a rare gem of gold inside of you and until you dig deep it would remain undiscovered because you do not find gold on the surface of the earth. Now when you discover gold in its natural state you need to purify and refine it to bring out the beauty in it. Until gold is refined you can't appreciate the beauty and the value of it.

So is talents, the moment you discover your talents, it is now left to you to purify and refine it in order to make it valuable. For instance if you can sing very well, you need to work and refine / enhance your vocals in order to be a world class singer. But if all you do is to look into your mirror and sing yourself happy everyday, then i am afraid that you are going nowhere to happen. All the worlds talented musicians improved and worked on their talents to be the worlds best. This formula is applicable to all fields as well.

Very importantly, you have to learn to trade your talent into cash. If your talent is singing, then trade it by selling records of your song, if your talent is acting, then trade it into cash, if it is making clothes, trade it into cash. Do not allow it to remain fallow. People have made millions of money just by turning their talents into cash. We have people like Angelina Jolie, Micheal Jackson, Dolly Patron, Naomi Campel Joan Collins, Cece Winas, Yolanda Adams and the list is endless.

Finally to enjoy success in anything you set out to do, remember that motivation is a necessary element. You don't have to be highly motivated, but at least a degree of motivation / interest is required without which failure is inevitable.

Motivation is what gets you started, habits is what keeps you going.

Jim Ryun.

If you love what you are doing, you will be successful.

Albert Schweitzer.

Your passion is a pointer to the problems you are created to solve.

Mike Murdock.

(32)

DECISION MAKING.

Todays decision are tommorow's realities.

Make a decision and watch your life move forward.
                                    Oprah Winfrey.

Decision making is a very vital part of our daily lives. Right from the moment we get up from our beds until the moment we drift up to sleep, we take decisions. Whether we like it or not we must take decisions. The fact that you took your bath in the morning, was a decision and it was a positive one, you could have decided not to take your bath at all. Our lives are filled with decisions and how far we go in life is based on the quality of decisions we make.

Your decision would determine the choices you make. Your decision could affect you positively or negatively. In life there are some serious decisions you must take, decisions such as who to marry, the choice of school, the choice of career, the home to buy, etc. In this type of decision, you do not apply the rule of thumb, or go about it with your head knowledge or human calculations.

The bible says there is a way that seems right, but the end of it is destruction...

Yes it may seem right physically, but in the realm of the spirit it is not right. It seemed right for Jacob to chose Rachel as his wife, but that did not seem right in the eyes of God. In the eyes of God Leah was the right one. Jacob never understood this until much later in his life that he understood that Leah was the right person for him. And one of his death wishes was that he should be buried beside his wife Leah. He never asked to buried alongside Rachel. Why!. Because Jacob later found out that Rachel loved worshipping idols.

Despite knowing Jacobs love for God, she still ignored this and clung onto the idols of her fathers house. When Jacob and all his household departed, Rachel stole the idols and took it along with her so that she can continue worshipping them.

And Laban, Rachel's father when he found out, that his idols were stolen was so furious and he came running after Jacob in search of his idols. This did not deter Rachel, and she clung unto the idols by hiding them when a search was carried out. That was how much she loved the idols and was never ready to give it out.

Now, Jacob was so sure that no one in his household would ever worship idols, not when they knew his love for God. Jacob was so confident that he beat his chest boldly and placed a curse on whoever stole them. Little did he know that the love of his life, the one whom he so much loved and slaved 14 years for, was the not only a schemer but a lover of idols, an idol worshipper and an expert liar. What a disappointment. And along the way Rachel died, it was then it dawned on Jacob what Rachel had done. He therefore concluded to be united in death with Leah whom he hated while she was alive.

So at times what seem right, may not be right, therefore,

"We should trust in the Lord with all our heart and lean not on your own understanding, in all our ways we should acknowledge him and he shall direct our path."

(Prov 3 v 5).

Also we should seek godly counsel. "In the multitude of counsellors, there is safety". Proverbs 15 v 22.

Surround yourself with godly people and seek their advice on certain issues of concern to you. Please make sure they are genuinely godly people before you even consult them. Look at their fruits, is their fruits testifying goodness?

Friends you do not and don't know it all. Everyday commit your ways and thoughts to him. God would definitely help you make the right decisions. Elijah was so dependent on God, that God even decided the food he would eat. God is interested in every area of your life. God took Elijah up into heaven he did not allow him to see death. So we must be like children in the hands of the potter. We must be suckling babes in the arms of God waiting daily watching at his gates to see and hear what he would say to us. Amen.

(33)

TAKE ACTION

Action is the key to success and failure to act is the reason most people will never achieve the kind of success they dream about.

Michael Masterson.

Action is the key to success, it is action that produces results. Success is not an accident. And success does not happen by chance. All successful people got themselves to consistently take effective actions toward the accomplishment of their dreams. If you don't take actions your ideas would always be unfulfilled dreams. You must take the type of action you believe will create the greatest probability of producing the result you desire.

You can have all the beautiful dreams and visions, but if you don't take action, your dreams will certainly die. Taking action is a necessity, it is not optional and it is vital as breathing in oxygen.

There was a young Jewish boy who had a vision of being the best or one of the best filmmakers in history. At the very tender age of 17 years he swung into action. He went to Universal studios and took a tour of it. It did not end there, he pursued his dream and continue to take action as the years rolled by, until he was offered a seven year contract to direct a T.V series. The rest is history. Today he is the best and most successful filmmaker in history. He made his dream come true by taking ACTION. He is no other than the one and only Steven Spielberg,

Most people look up and admire the stars. A champion climbs a mountain and grabs one. Therefore action always precedes results. Rise up and give life to that dream, that vision by taking action. NOW IS THE WORD. Winning starts with beginning.

On the shores of hesitation lies the bones of countless millions, who at the dawn of success waited and while waiting died.

Robert Schuler.

Most people live and die with their music still un played. They never dare try.

Mary Kay Ash.

They are many rules for success, but none of them will work unless you do.

Read Markham.

The most wonderful thing that can happen to a dream is a specific plan of action.

Myles Munroe.

You wont win if you don't begin.

Robert Schuler.

⊙⊙⊙⊙⊙

(34)

YOU NEED WISDOM.

"Wisdom is supreme, therefore seek wisdom"
Proverbs 4 v 7.

In this world prevalent with evil, you need wisdom to survive.

The habitation of the world is filled with wickedness, evil people everywhere therefore you need wisdom to prevail.

By wisdom a house is built and through understanding it is established, through knowledge its rooms are filled with rare and beautiful treasures.

Above all else you need wisdom. Ask God for wisdom. Without wisdom life would be tough, because you are dealing and living in a world system filled with lots of evil people who are full off evil imaginations.

Let us look at the story of Samson who was highly anointed, in fact he was a star right from birth. However he lacked the wisdom to deal with Delilah. Delilah was set up against him by his enemies and a silly question from this woman destroyed him.

Please note that Delilah did not hide or disguise her intention, as a matter of fact she made it plain to Samson that she was out to destroy him, by demonstrating it on two occasions when she called the Philistines to come and get him.

Samson saw all these and one would have thought that he would have immediately separated himself from this evil woman, and run for his dear life, but he lacked wisdom and could not use discretion, unfortunately he died and on the laps of this devilish woman. His great and colourful destiny came to an abrupt end due to lack of wisdom. What a waste.

"A wise man has great power and a man of knowledge increase strength, for waging war you need guidance."

(35)

LEARN TO BE HUMBLE.

"God resists the proud, but he gives grace to the humble."

James 4 v 6.

"The Lord detest all the proud of heart. Be sure of this they would not go unpunished." Proverbs 16 v 5.

The opposite of humility is pride. What is pride.

Pride is feeling that you are better than anyone else. Pride is having an haughty spirit.

God can't abide with a proud person. The first trace of pride was recorded when Lucifer became proud in his heart and wanted to set himself above God his maker, he paid the full price for it and he lost his place in heaven forever and ever.

Beloved in all you do, never ever be proud. You may ask or think within yourself that you are not proud, well I would suggest you do a checklist of the following to see if you fall into any of the category.

A. **When you are so conscious of your self esteem.** You are more interested in your image making than anything else. King Saul is an example of this. He regarded his self esteem more than God. He was always conscious of his image, what people thought of him and he always tried to please people at the expense of his relationship with God. We can see this in 1st Samuel 15 v 1- 34, God instructed Saul to go and destroy the Amalekites and all they had.

Saul disobeyed God and did not carry out the whole instructions. Now Samuel approached Saul and told him how God was displeased with him.

And rather than Saul to feel sorry for his actions and ask God for forgiveness, he was rather interested in his image making in front of the Israelites. He never felt the need to repent and when Samuel turned to go away, one would have thought Saul would ask for forgiveness, but rather this is what he said in 1st Samuel 15 v 26, 30;

Saul replied, I have sinned, BUT PLEASE HONOR ME BEFORE THE ELDERS OF ISRAEL; COME BACK WITH ME, so that I may worship the Lord YOUR GOD."

What a shame, do we see the havoc pride can cause, this is a king who had just been told that God was displeased with him, and all he can think of was his self esteem, his royal image. He had to beg Samuel to honour him before the elders of Israel by coming back to worship God with him. He chose his self image/ reputation over his relationship with God. If we compare him with King David who was humble, we can see a wide margin of difference between them.

B. **When you keep sinning and refuse to repent, this condescends into iniquity.** A heart that refuse to repent is a proud heart. God can not dwell with a proud heart. When you continue in your sin, day in day out and refuse to repent amounts to taking God for granted. The book of Judges 16 v 1 - 31, tells us about the story of Samson. Samson was a highly anointed man of God and God used him for great exploits. However he had a weakness for sexual immorality. He kept on sinning and sinning without repenting and God departed from him because God can not dwell with anyone who take him for granted. Please do not take God for granted. In as much as God is a God of mercy, he is also a God of Judgement. Shall we continue in sin that grace may abound.

"So the rulers of the Philistines returned with the silver in their hands. Having put him to sleep on her lap, she called a man to shave off the seven braids of his hair, and began to subdue him. And his strength left him. Then she called, Samson, the Philistines are upon you.

He awoke from his sleep and thought, I WILL GO
OUT AS BEFORE AND SHAKE MYSELF FREE,
BUT HE DID NOT KNOW THAT THE LORD
HAD LEFT HIM." Judges 16 v 18 - 20.

C. If you do not show reverence for God or the things of God.

In the book of Daniel 5 v 1- 30, tells us about a king
called Belshazzar who had no reverence for God. His
heart rose up in pride and he ordered the gold goblets
to be brought from the temple of God and he, his wives
and concubines drank wine from it and he praised the
gods of silver and gold without honouring God. God
immediately pronounced judgement on him. That very
night he was slain to death.

Friends our God is a God full of mercy, but he is also a
God of judgement.

D. When you speak or act in defiance against constituted authority, both in the Church and in the society.

Acting in the above way builds rebellion and rebellion
is as the sin of witchcraft. It was rebellion that brought
down lucifer. lucifer formerly held an exalted position,
but he became rebellious and was thrown out of heaven.

Please pray over those God has chosen as leaders and
don't speak against them carelessly, or be rebellious

against them. Rather the bible enjoins us to pray for them. There is nothing wrong in airing your views, but it must be done constructively and honestly, rather than taking the back bench and criticising them. God cannot stand rebellious people.

Miriam spoke against Moses and God dealt with her. Korah, Dathan and Abiram spoke against Moses and they died an unusual death

E. When you feel you are better than everyone. You refuse to be corrected, you are arrogant.

The Pharisees felt they were better because they followed the law of Moses, this resulted in them have a haughty spirit and made them to reject the Messiah.

F. The moment you begin to use the phrase I WILL DO THIS, I WILL THAT. Please watch it, because you are beginning to be self conceited and this is a key ingredient of pride. This was the same language that the devil used and it cost him his place in heaven forever and ever.

The devil said in Isaiah 14 v 13,

"I WILL ascend to heaven,
I WILL raise my throne above the stars of God,
I WILL sit enthroned on the mount of assembly.
I WILL ascend above the tops of the clouds,
I WILL make myself like the Most High."

G. When you think highly of yourself.

King Nebuchadnezzar in Daniel 4 v 1 - 36 thought highly of himself and became proud, God humbled him.

Beloved these are reflective moments and it is advisable to sit back and go over your life, your attitude, character seriously. Please do not be casual about this, because pride is very subtle and you might not even know or think you are proud.

Lets us take an example of one person who was proud, but never knew until his time of testing and trials came and that is the person of Job.

In Job 30 v 1 this is what Job said "But now they mock me, men younger than I, whose fathers I would have disdained to put with my sheep dogs."

Who would have thought, Job can utter this statement, for out of the abundance of the heart, the mouth speaks.

Beloved, do not get carried away with the subtility of pride, if you think you have any of these elements of pride in you, then it is time to adjust. Rise up and chase away the little foxes that can ruin the vineyard. As long as those foxes remain, they would hamper your success.

Friends, it is time to adjust and quietly repent in your heart, because you never know. Some people may be wondering why success is not answering to them or why they are facing hardship. Who knows, maybe there is an element of pride. Because God would always resists the proud.

Friends, how can you succeed in this dark world if God is not on your side.

(36)

DONT ENTERTAIN FAILURE.

You may have to fight a battle more than once to win.
Magaret Thatcher.

Successful people don't entertain failure, it doesn't exist in their dictionary, they only refer to failure as an outcome or a result and they try again and again until they get their desired results. People who believe in failure or entertain failure are almost guaranteed a mediocre existence. People who achieve greatness do not perceive failure. They don't dwell on it, neither do they attach negative emotions to something that doesn't work. They keep trying and trying until they achieve their desired results.

Abraham Lincoln was one of the finest president America ever produced, yet he failed many times at election. However he never entertained this defeat called failure and he kept trying and trying until he finally won the election and was sworn in as president of the United States of America.

Similarly all the world class inventors who invented most of the amenities we are enjoying today, never entertained failure at all, not even for one second. We have the Wright brothers who invented the airplane amidst several records of failure.

Also there was a man called Thomas Edison, after he had tried 9,999 times to perfect the light bulb and hadn't succeeded someone asked him "Are you going to have ten thousand failures. He answered I didn't fail, I just discovered another way not to invent the electric bulb."
As far as he was concerned there was no room for failure, so he kept on trying new methods until he finally came up with the perfect results he wanted. And here we are today, all enjoying the results.

According to Oprah Winfrey, the second richest and most successful black woman on planet earth has this to say,

I will tell you that there has been no failures in my life, but there have been some tremendous lessons.
Oprah Winfrey.

Please going forward always have this at the back of your mind, that if you try something and you don't get the outcome you desire, consider it simply as feedback, wipe the word failure from your dictionary / memory. Keep trying different methods until you get your desired results. As the saying goes you can't keep trying something the same way and you expect different results. Also we all learn from our mistakes or the mistakes of others. Experience they say is the best teacher, but I would say if you consider your mistakes as failures, then you are going nowhere to happen, rather see your mistakes as lessons to be learnt and don't repeat them again.

Every man fails, champions simply get up and begin again.
                                        Myles Munroe.

Success will only smile at the man who refuses to lie down at the corridor of failure.

                                        Myles Munroe.

(37)

THE POWER OF BELIEVING.

What you believe has more power than what you dream or wish or hope for. You become what you believe.
Oprah Winfrey.

The word believing is a continuous present tense. That is, it is always in the present and does not dwell in the past, it is also always on going, very active and resides in the present. It is not enough to only believe yesterday, no, you have to keep believing to the next moment, to the nearest future and on and on.

Believing is the catalyst you need to activate your success. If you don't believe you would succeed then you won't succeed. Excuse me to say or to use this illustration, a thief that sets out to steal, is always believing that he would not get caught, even after he has stolen he still carries on believing that he would never ever get caught and with this mindset he carries on stealing. (I do not advocate stealing, but I am only using it to pass across the whole idea of what believing is). It is your believe in the success of whatever you lay your hands upon that would keep you going even if you have just encountered a several massive bouts of defeat. The power of believing is so strong that it directs your whole course of action and allows you to produce remarkable and outstanding results.

A classical example of continuous believing is taken from the book of Job in the bible. Here was a man who had lost everything he ever had, his children, wealth etc. Even his health was attacked, he had sores all over his body, but one thing that kept him going was the power of believing. He did not allow his circumstances to determine the state of his thinking. His mind was very intact and his thoughts was always inclined to keep believing positively that one day his change will come. And this is what he had to say in,

Job 14 v 14 *I will wait for my change to come.*

And in Job 19 v 25, Job says,

I know that my redeemer lives and that in the end he will stand upon the earth.
And after my skin has been destroyed, yet in my flesh I will see God,
I myself will see him, with my own eyes, I not another.

And eventually Job saw God.

Then Job replied to the Lord,
My ears had heard of you,
But now my eyes have seen you.

Job 42 v 5.

Furthermore the opposite of continuous believing is continuous doubting. There is nothing that punctures a colourful destiny as doubts. Doubt is an enemy you should try very hard not to entertain. Don't open your door to let it in, because it is an unfavourable guest. It is also a potential enemy. Doubt will rob you of success. Successful people never accommodate doubt, they see everything as possible. They keep on believing and believing.

He who doubts is a double minded man, unstable in all his ways.

James 1 v 8.

Nothing ruins ones destiny like doubt and unbelief.
Benson Idahosa.

Our doubts are traitors, and make us lose the good we oft might win, by fearing to attempt.
William Shakespeare.

(38)

ACCEPT RESPONSIBILTY.

Success on any major scale requires you to accept responsibility in the final analysis. The one quality that all successful people have is the ability to take on responsibility.

Michael Korda.

You can blame everyone, your parents, friends, acquaintances and so on for your past, but can't blame anyone for your future. You and no one is absolutely responsible for your future.

You are the determinant of your future.

Enoch Adeboye.

Therefore wake up, give up the blame game and begin to take full responsibility.

At the garden of Eden, Adam blamed everybody but himself. Eve took full responsibility. Maybe that's why

God loves women. (Laugh it off, author is just being humorous).

Those who take responsibility are always in charge and they quickly look for solutions. People who pass the buck by always blaming others hardly progress neither do they make any meaningful headway in life. Why, because they are busy looking at others and pointing fingers at them, rather than focusing on themselves and looking inwards. The answer or solution does not lie in pointing fingers at others, but the solution lies in your hands and no one else.

Don't find fault, find a remedy.
Henry Ford.

THE ENEMY CALLED FEAR.

Fear not, for I have redeemed you, I have summoned you by name. When you pass through the waters, I will be with you. When you walk through the fire, you will not be burned.

Isaiah 43 v 1 -2.

Fear is a feeling, an emotion you have to learn to overcome. In all you do, don't entertain fear. There is nothing that poisons the mind as fear, fear is one of the greatest limitations for majority of people. When we store negative emotions, we affect our physiology, our thinking process and this takes a toll on our actions.

What would you attempt to do, if you knew, you could not fail.
Robert Schuller.

Fear is a negative feeling you have, regarding something. To further understand fear, you have to know where it stems from. Man is tripartite, that is made up of body, soul and spirit. The body is the flesh, the container. The soul is the emotions and feelings side, whilst the spirit is the life itself. Fear emanates from the flesh, from what you see, hear or think and this goes further to control your feelings and emotions, thereby affecting your spirit man. Your spirit man ought to act as a resistance, but if you allow your emotions and feelings to control your actions, then there is little or nothing the spirit man can do. That is why we have to feed our spirit man with, the word of God, with prayer, and with fasting.

To overcome fear, you have to build your faith and learn not to walk by what you see, but you have to walk by the word of God.

Everyone was afraid of Goliath, his size alone was terrifying. But only one man could look at Goliath and challenge him. Why? David did not look at the intimidating size of Goliath, rather he focused on the bigness and mightiness of God. Therefore, anytime you are faced with a challenge and fear wants to set in always do yourself a big favour and imagine how big God is, the heavens can't contain God, the clouds are the dust of his feet, the earth is his footstool, God is the sole commander of the entire universe, God alone holds the breath of every mankind in his hand. He is the King of Kings and Lord of Lords. So, why fear?

Therefore going forward, never entertain fear anymore, rather focus on the bigness of God and all iota of fear would automatically be wiped off.

Impossibility vanished when a man and his God confront a mountain.

Annoymous.

(40)

THE POWER OF INFORMATION.

Formal education will make you a living, self education will make you a fortune.

Jim Rohn.

My people perish for lack of knowledge.

Hosea 4 v 6.

Knowledge is an antidote to ignorance. Ignorance as they say is not an excuse. For the information or knowledge you don't know, you will pay dearly for it. Knowledge wipes away ignorance.

There is no mountain anywhere, everybody's mountain is his ignorance.

David Oyedepo.

Knowledge is power. For instance an aspiring student who wants to be a medical doctor, must go to college and get the necessary knowledge to qualify as a doctor. Likewise a business man who wants to go into any particular area of business must go and acquire information. You can't be ignorant in a particular area and expect to succeed. Its just not possible. Also you can't stop not learning, because the world we live in, is very dynamic. There are always new information, new techniques and so on. Therefore you have to avail yourself of all these avalanches of information and increase your knowledge.

Empower yourself today and seek knowledge. Knowledge empowers your mind. Your mind is the greatest determinant of your destiny. According to Oprah Winfrey, the 2nd richest black woman on planet earth, she attributes her wealth to the knowledge she gained from reading books.

Books were my pass to personal freedom. I learned to read at age three and there discovered was a whole world to conquer that went beyond our farm in Mississipi.

Oprah Winfrey.

Some women have a weakness for shoes, i can go barefoot if necessary. i have a weakness for books.

Oprah Winfrey.

When i didn't have friends, i had books.

Oprah Winfrey.

Whatever you would become starts from your mind. Therefore feed your mind with the right information and the result would always be positive. To achieve greatness therefore feed your mind with information on greatness / success and automatically you will start doing things that reflect greatness and the results would be success all round. According to one of the living legends of our time, he says and I quote.

The mind can be likened to the control room of life, because it co-ordinates and controls the activities of man.
Your mind is the gateway to your life.
What you will become in life must be seen in your mind.
                                                    David Oyedepo.

You are what you are and you are where you are because of what has gone into your mind.
                                                    Zig Ziglar.

All I have learned, I have learned from books.
                                                    Abraham Lincoln.

Rich people have small T.V and big libraries and poor people have small libraries and big T.V's.
                                                    Zig Ziglar.

You can shrug your shoulders and say you are not a fan of reading, yes you may not be a fan of reading, but there are several other ways of getting information. You can listen to DVD's, MP'3, watch videos, attend seminars, interact with successful people, listen to motivational speakers and a whole lot. Where there is a will, there is way. Hear this, with the right information and knowledge at your disposal, you can become anything you want to be. Therefore don't rest on your oars, go out there and empower yourself with the necessary information.

Finally, i conclude with this

THE POWER OF IDEAS.

All achievements, all earned riches have their beginning in an idea.
Napoleon Hill.

Nothing on earth is more powerful than an idea. Everything in this life started from an idea. All the greatest inventions that the world has ever witnessed all came about as a result of someones idea, someones thought. Ideas produce everything. Your idea will outlive you if it is successful. Example is the Wright brothers who while watching birds fly, had an idea of an aircraft that will carry human beings and as a result of that singular idea, here we are today several years later, still benefiting from that idea. Also Thomas Edison, the man who invented the light bulb.

Also the talented Steve Jobs of blessed memory whose idea it was that gave us APPLE technology and the list is endless. Even in death Steve Jobs idea is still selling like hotcake and is yielding him millions of dollars in the grave. These all had wonderful ideas. If they could do it, you also can do it. In the body of Christ we need people with great ideas, whose ideas will churn out such a great amount of wealth. We have left it to long for unbelievers, it is now time for every christian to arise and put on their thinking caps and begin to think of great ideas, money spinning ideas.

As a child of God, we should be the ones to come up with mind blowing ideas. Why? because we have the Holy Spirit in us. We have the power of God inside us.

HOW DO WE GET IDEAS.

1. Inspiration

This can be drawn from many sources, such as mother nature, music, social interaction, reading etc. However as a child of God you have the greatest access to inspiration. You should not lack ideas. Why? because according to Job 32 v 8 it says,

But there is a spirit in a man, the breath of the Almighty that gives him understanding. (Inspiration)

Therefore as a child of God the spirit of God is in you via the Holy Spirit, hence you should not lack ideas at all.

2. Meditation

This means to carefully go over something in your mind over and over again.

In Joshua 1 v 8, we see God commanding Joshua on what to do in order to have success.

This book of the law shall not depart from your mouth, meditate on it day and night, then you shall have great SUCCESS.

As you meditate on God's word, you will get divine ideas, that will be of immense benefit to the body of Christ and the entire world.

3. Strategic Thinking

This is when you focus your attention, on a particular subject or area of concern. By so doing, a solution will arise.

4. Brain Storming

What you do here is go over an issue over and over again. Weigh the pros and cons, to look for a way out, in the midst of that, ideas will erupt suddenly.

5. Quietness

Elijah was one man who always adopted this method. You have to develop your spirit man to maintain quietness. It does not pay to be noisy all the time. Excuse me to say that most Christians are too noisy, too busy talking and talking. Unfortunately they carry this attitude to their prayer closet, they talk and talk without learning the art of waiting to hear from God. We have the Holy Spirit as a gift to us and he is with us to speak to us and give us directions, but how many people are hearing him? Please going forward, learn to maintain a quiet spirit and you will be amazed at what your spirit man receives inwardly from the Holy Spirit. Sometimes it is in the midst of quietness that you hear the voice of God clearly giving you directions on what to do. Being quiet does not mean you should not talk, but it means that you maintain calmness within you, so that you can be attentive and listen out for the voice of God.

Here are some powerful life changing quotes, which will revolutionize your thinking and change your life forever. Success does not come from where you are, but from the way you think. Visualize success and you will achieve it.

Man was designed for accomplishment, engineered and endowed with the seed of greatness.

Zig Ziglar.

I never learn anything talking. I only learn things when I ask questions.

Lou Holtz.

Never give up, for that is just the place and time that the tide will turn forever.

Harriet Beecher Stowe.

No bird soars too high if he soars with his own wings.
William Blake.

There is always room at the top.

Daniel Webster.

There are two ways to open a door. You either have the keys to open it nicely or you force it open by breaking it.

Annoymous.

You don't have to be great to start, but you have to start to be great.

Zig Ziglar.

People do not wander and find themselves at the top of Mt Everest.

Zig Ziglar.

Great faith is the product of great fights. Great testimonies are the outcome of great tests. Great triumphs can only come out of great trials.

Smith Wigglesworth.

Our confession will either imprison us or set us free. Our confession is the result of our believing and our believing is the result of our right or wrong thinking.

Kenneth Haggin.

You can foul up the devil's whole strategy by taking charge of your thoughts and bring them in line with the word of God.

Kenneth Copeland.

Both poverty and riches are the offspring of the thought.

Napoleon Hill.

More gold has been taken from the thoughts of men than has been taken from the earth.

Napoleon Hill.

You can't cross the sea by merely standing and staring at the water.

Norman Vincent Peale.

Life has no return match.

David Oyedepo.

You are either running with a vision, going on a mission or burning with passion. If you don't belong to any of these life is reduced to a burden.

David Oyedepo.

If you must make a difference in life, then change your mind set.

Matthew Ashimolowo.

When you give the devil attention, he will give you direction.

Benson Idahosa.

The best way to predict your future is to create it.

Abraham Lincoln.

Silence cannot be misquoted.

Myles Munroe.

When you get to the end of your rope. Tie a knot and hang on.

Franklin D. Roosevelt.

My great concern is not whether you have failed, but whether you are content with your failure.

Abraham Lincoln.

The graveyard is the richest place on the surface of the earth, because there you will see the books that were not yet published, ideas that were not harnessed, songs that were not sung and drama pieces that were never acted.

Myles Munroe.

Difficulties break some men, but make others.
                                Nelson Mandela.

Don't dream of winning, train to win.
                                Mo Farah.

Just because you go to church doesn't mean you are a Christian. I can go sit in the garage all day and it doesn't make me a car.
                                Joyce Meyer.

Don't run to the phone, run to the throne.
                                Joyce Meyer.

Never talk defeat, use words like hope, belief, faith, victory.
                                Norman Vincent Peale.

Lack of direction, not lack of time is the problem. We all have 24 hour days.
                                Zig Ziglar

When obstacles arise you change your direction to reach your goal, you do not change your decision to get there.
                                Zig Ziglar.

We live in a thinkers world. Thinkers rule the world. If you are not a thinker you end up as a slave.
                                David Oyedepo.

Our past may explain why we are suffering, but we must not use it as an excuse to stay in bondage.
                                Joyce Meyer.

One mistake does not have to ruin a person's entire life.
Joyce Meyer.

I am a slow walker, but I never walk backwards.
Abraham Lincoln.

God never consult your past to determine your future.
Myles Munroe.

The day you make a decision about your life is the day your life your world will change.
Mike Murdock.

Some blessings can not locate you except you are clothed in the cotton and linen of humility.
Enoch Adeboye.

Don't limit yourself. Many people limit themselves to what they think they can do. You can go as far as your mind let you. What you believe you can achieve.
Mary Kay Ash.

Any fact facing us is not as important as our attitude toward it, for that determines our success or failure.
Norman Vincent Peale.

Some people dream of success, while others wake up and work hard at it.
Annoymous.

The road to success runs uphill.
Willie Davis.

You can achieve anything you want, so long as you have faith in God, have faith in yourself, work hard and never let anyone tell you, you can't do something.
Elvis Presley

Stick to one thing until you succeed at it. Do not be discouraged and save, save save. Unless you practice thrift you can never become much. Lay aside every dollar you can and after a while you will have enough to start a business.
John D Rockefeller.

If A is success in life, then A equals X plus Y plus Z. Work is X, Y is play and Z is keeping your mouth shut.
Albert Einstein.

Do what you can, with what you have where you are.
Theodore Roosevelt.

Your life can't go according to plan, if you have no plan.
Zig Ziglar.

When you know the word of God it will change you.
Kenneth Haggin.

Always remember that your present situation is not your final destination, the best is yet to come.
Zig Ziglar.

When we face our fears we can find freedom.
Joyce Meyer.

If you cannot identify the appropriate key, you will be barred from entering your breakthrough.

Enoch Adeboye.

Anyone who does not contribute to your progress in any way is an excess luggage, drop the fellow.

Enoch Adeboye.

If you are trying to achieve, there will be road blocks. I have had them, everybody has had them. But obstacles don't have to stop you. If you run into a wall, don't turn around and give up. Figure out how to climb it, go through it or work around it.

Micheal Jordan.

The quickest way to success is to take the shortcut of developing and having the right mental attitude that the only way to get to the top of any mountain is to start climbing from the bottom.

Jemima Alara.

Get going, move forward. Aim high. Plan a take off. Don't just sit on the runaway and hope someone will come along and push the airplane. It simply won't happen. Change your attitude and gain some altitude. Believe me you will love it up there.

Donald Trump.

If you can be bought at whatever price you have lost your value.

Enoch Adeboye.

Be not afraid of greatness, some are born great, some achieve greatness and some have greatness thrust upon them.

William Shakespeare.

FOOTPRINTS ON THE SANDS OF TIME ARE NOT MADE BY SITTING DOWN.

BOOK TWO

THE RISE OF
THE EAGLE CHRISTIAN

JEMIMA ALARA

INTRODUCTION

God has called every christian to come and partake of his divine nature and attribute. One of this divine attribute is the attribute of an Eagle. Every child of God has been designed to live a colourful and enviable life. A life purposefully designed by God himself to show forth his glory through human vessels.

The Eagle is commonly known and referred to as the king of all birds. The eagle is a peculiar bird of an exceptional nature and uniqueness. Eagles are in a class of their own. Eagles display great amount of wisdom, knowledge and dominion. The eagle is fearless, bold and it can only be found in very high places.

Eagles understand vision and purpose and all through their life they run and live their lives according to their divine purpose and plan. Eagles do not live carelessly and you can never find them in the lower class or at the bottom. They are always on top, always the head.

It is this realm that God has called every christian to come and partake. And the scripture in 2nd Peter 1 v 3 – 4 confirms it,

"God's divine power has given us everything we need for life and godliness through the knowledge of him who called us by his glory and goodness. Through these he has given us his great precious promises, so that through them YOU MAY PARTICIPATE IN THE DIVINE NATURE and escape the corruption in the world.

⊙⊙⊙⊙⊙⊙

THERE IS AN EAGLE IN YOU.

"And we all, with unveiled face, beholding as in a mirror the glory of the Lord, are being transformed into the same image from glory to glory, which comes from the Lord, who is the Spirit."
2nd Corinthians 3 v 18.

The main essence of our salvation is to be transformed into the same image of our beloved Saviour Jesus Christ the Lord. Now Jesus Christ is awesome and he has so many wonderful attributes and description. The prophet Ezekiel gives us a description of God in Ezekiel 1 v 1 - 28.

In the thirtieth year, in the fourth month on the fifth day, while i was among the exiles by the Kebar river,
The heavens were opened and i saw visions of God.
I looked and I saw a windstorm coming out of the north.
An immense cloud with flashing lightening surrounded by brilliant light.
The center of the fire looked like glowing metal.

And in the fire was what looked like four living creatures.
In appearance their form was that of a man.
But each of them had four faces and four wings.
Under their wings on their four sides they had the
hands of a man.
All four of them had faces and wings and their wings
touched one another.
Their faces looked like this.
Each of the four had the face of a man,
And on the right side, each had the face of a lion.
And on the left, the face of an ox.
Each also had the face of an eagle.
This was the appearance of the likeness of the glory
of God.
When i saw it I fell face down, and i heard a voice of
one speaking.
This was the appearance of the likeness of the glory of
the Lord. When I saw it I fell facedown, and I heard
the voice of one speaking.

Also in Revelation 4 v 1-11, John was taken up into the
spirit and he saw the glory of God.

After this I looked and there before me was a door
standing open in heaven.
At once I was in the spirit and there before me a door
standing open in heaven with someone sitting on it.
In the center around the throne,
Were four living creatures and they were covered with
eyes in front and back.
The first living creature was like a lion,
The second was like an ox,
The third had the face like a man,
The fourth was like a flying eagle.

Now from the above two scriptures we are given a brief description of God's image as he appeared to Ezekiel and John. The images are,

1. MAN
2. EAGLE
3. OX
4. LION

The bible tells us that the intention of God was to create man, you and I in his own image. And we can see this in Genesis 1 v 26- 27 *"Then God said, Let us make man in our image, in our likeness.*

So God created man in his own image, in the image of God he created him, male and female he created them."

Whoa! what a superstar you are. You are fearfully and wonderfully made and God has called all his children to partake of his attributes. In the beginning Adam manifested all the divine attribute of God, he had dominion over all what God created, he was bold as a lion, he was cruising on a high altitude in the realms of glory as an eagle, he displayed much strength because he was never tired, can you imagine what it was like to take care and be in charge of the whole earth, the sea, the birds of the air, etc, Adam was simply in a class of his own. However, sin eroded man of this splendid nature and separated man from partaking of this divine nature, but Jesus Christ came to restore us back to God and give us what Adam had lost. Now then, we have the opportunity given to us to get back to our original position, back to Eden, back to God's original purpose of creating man. We were created after the image and likeness of God. And the image of God as described in the above scriptures includes, LION, OX, EAGLE and MAN.

It is pertinent to note that everyone born into this world has the first attribute and that is the attribute of a MAN, and we are left with the other three. However this other three attributes which is EAGLE, OX AND LION is not for everyone, because Adam lost it and we can only gain it back through Christ Jesus. Jesus came to restore man back to his original position. As Jesus is, so are we. And we are expected to attain the full image of Christ, please take note of the word ATTAIN. This means it is not automatic and we have to do something to get it. We have to be born again, born of water and spirit. Not everyone attains, because it is not everyone that receives Jesus, by accepting to be born again,

"Yet to all who received him, to those who believed in his name, he gave the right to become children of God."
1st John 1 v 12.

Therefore until you receive Christ as your Lord and saviour you can never attain the remaining three attributes. That is EAGLE, LION AND OX.

It is only in Christ Jesus that we can manifest the remaining 3 attributes. Without Christ we can never and no one can ever manifest it. It is when we come to Christ that we receive the power of the Holy Spirit and it is the Holy Spirit in us that will activate these potentials already in us. You are to be a wonder in this world, not a wonder by the clothes you wear nor by the political or career heights you attain, but you are wonder by the manifestation of the potentials inside of you.

You are to fly as an eagle,

You are to rule and have dominion over the earth,

You are to be bold and fearless like a lion,

You are to be as strong as an ox.

It is when you are living out these potentials inside of you then you can be deemed to be a wonder to your generation.

The creation is waiting for the whole manifestation of the children of God.

Romans 8 v 31.

Beloved the world is waiting for your manifestation. Enough of holding back and living a life of limitation, enough of living below the belt, take the limits off and rise above the limits, rise like an eagle and get ready to soar high. High into realms of glory, from glory to glory.

Who are these that fly along like clouds, like doves to their nests.
Isaiah 60 v 8.

Beloved you are too much, God has designed you to be a super star, a star to your generation, stop living the life of average Joe, you are to be the light of this world, you are like a city which is set on the hill and can't be hidden. There is a deposit inside of you, do not let the devil use the tool of ignorance to rob you of this priceless treasure embedded in you.

Hear this inside of you are these four potentials,

1) Man----Ruler, dominion.

2) Eagle---King of all birds.
3) Ox------Burden bearer, known for exceptional
strength.
4) Lion-----King of all animals.

What a package with such wonderful contents. Friends you are wonderfully and fearfully made. Be that as it may, until you discover your contents, you can never know your value and worth.

Imagine you have a gift of an aircraft, and everyday all you do is to admire it. Forever that aircraft will just be an object to be admired. However the day you are able to discover the purpose, contents and function of that aircraft, you will gladly hop into it and begin flying all around the world.

Similarly, there was this story of a baby eaglet that fell off from it's nest to the ground. It landed among chickens and it began living with the chickens. As time went by, it did everything the chickens did, such as scrambling the earth for food, lazying around and burrowing in the sand most of the day. Meanwhile this eaglet is a prospective eagle and it was not created to be a chicken but circumstances made it think and believe that it was a chicken. It had the potentials of an eagle inside of it, but it did not know. Friends that is how most Christians are living their lives. Majority of Christians don't know the potentials embedded in them and they just go through life casually with a lackadaisical attitude.

Well, the tables turned in favour of this eaglet when one day an old farmer was passing by. The farmer was very disturbed to see an eaglet in the midst of chickens scrambling for food. With so much anger inside of the farmer, the farmer quickly grabbed this eaglet and took the eaglet to a very high cliff. At the cliff, he threw the eaglet down, the eaglet was so terrified, and it started struggling. In a bid to stay alive, the eaglet realized it could flap it's wings and it started doing so. Gradually it realized it could fly and it began flying and it flew and flew until it soared high into the clouds. What a happy day for that eaglet.

Beloved that is how God wants all his children to be, to fly high and not to remain at the bottom scrambling for food. You have to yearn to bring out and maximize the potentials inside of you to the highest level. Therefore, until you discover the contents you are made of, you will continue limiting yourself. Discovery leads to revelation and with revelation comes illumination. Enough of living below the belt. Enough of living like a victim, it is time to live like a victor.

Your time has come to shine, there is an eagle in you, stop living like a chicken, chicken's never fly they are always found on the ground, found at the bottom, at the tail position in life. And this is in sharp contrast with the word of God in Deut 28 v 13 which says You shall be the head and not the tail. How can one be the head as a chicken. Chickens are destined for the bottom, they never fly. As long as one refuses to rise up and soar as an eagle the tail position is inevitable. Enough is enough, it is time to unleash the eagle in you, it is time to soar high, high above the clouds. Let the eagle in you arise.

For in Christ Jesus all the fullness of the deity lives in bodily form and you have been given fullness in Christ, who is the head over every power and authority.
2nd Colossians 2 v 9-10.

For the purposes of this book we shall be looking at God's attribute from the perspective of an EAGLE.

ᏯᏯᏯᏯᏯ

BRINGING OUT THE EAGLE IN YOU.

Furthermore, God has called all his children to be Eagles. The most notable feature of Eagles is that they only dwell in high places and they live exceptionally unique lifestyle that is second to none. God has already deposited in us what it takes for us to live on high.

"And God raised us up with Christ and seated us with him in heavenly realms in Christ Jesus. "Ephesians 2v 6.

When we newly receive Christ at new birth (salvation) we are referred to as babies in the Lord and we are expected to grow in the Lord. "Like newborn babies you should crave the pure spiritual milk, that by it you may be nurtured and grow unto completed salvation." 1st Peter 2 v 2.

Just like a Christian at new birth is referred to as a babe, so is an eagle at birth referred to as an eaglet. The eaglet has to grow to become an eagle. Unfortunately not every eaglet becomes an eagle, so also it is not every Christian that grows into full maturity into the image of Christ. Some eaglets lose their identity and die as chickens, so also do some Christians lose their identity, they never discover who they are in Christ and they die as chickens.

This is not the will and desire of God for us, God wants us to develop our wings from being baby Christians (eaglets) to become Eagles (matured Christians). Eaglet's always stay in their nest because there are babies, they refuse to mature. Gods desire is for us not to remain in the nest, he wants us to come out of the nest and learn to fly and then finally soar. The ultimate for every eaglet's is to soar high.

"You shall mount with wings as a eagle." Isaiah 40 v 31b.

Also a child as long as he is a child would remain subject to guardians and servants. He can't ascend the throne, regardless of the fact that he is right beside the throne. However the moment he comes of age (maturity level), then he can ascend the throne. God's desire is for us to ascend the throne. He wants us to grow and attain maturity to the nature of Christ.

"Until Christ be formed in us." Galatians 4 v 19.

Unfortunately many Christians remain eaglets all their lives and that is not God's will for us. His will is that we grow and attain the full stature of Christ.

"Until we all reach unity in the faith and in the knowledge of the Son of God and become mature, attaining to the whole measure of the fullness of Christ."

Ephesians 4 v 13.

Beloved, it is very risky to remain as an eaglet, as a baby Christian because we live in a world where evil is so prevalent. The bible says in Psalm 74 v 20 that the dark places of the world is filled with the habitation of cruelty."

The risk associated with being an eaglet is

(1) One could fall out of the nest to the ground. And this is a reality because some eaglets do actually fall out of their nest. And when that happens one becomes a chicken. The consequences of this is death, both physically and spiritually.

(2) Starvation which would lead to loss of status and identity, because eaglets can not fend for themselves so they would eat anything available just to survive.

(3) One would suffer stagnancy and remain on the same spot, because the eaglet has not learned how to fly yet.

(4) Powerless, one can not walk in the supernatural lying on the ground.

(5) You become an easy prey for the devil.

(6) The chances of backsliding is highly likely.

(7) You become vulnerable.

Now you are faced with a choice, to remain an eaglet or to be an eagle.

God has given us all choices. And the choice is yours.

Also if you choose to be an eagle Christian then you are admonished to be perfect as Christ is and to walk as Christ walked, so that greater works than Christ did shall you do also. Therefore to be an eagle Christian, you need to have all the attributes an eagle possesses. So, what makes an eagle unique and special. Let's find out and I pray that as you read along, you would develop and encapsulate yourself with all the wonderful qualities that makes an Eagle an Eagle. Amen.

16 QUALITIES THAT MAKES AN EAGLE AN EAGLE.

---

(1)

EAGLES DO NOT FLOCK.

--Eagles never flock together as compared to birds who flock together. Eagles move about and fly alone and they also select the tallest trees of the forest, the topmost cray of the mountain and live alone in solitude. They also hunt and feed alone.

As believers the moment we become born again, we are expected to seperate ourselves from the world, by doing the following,

1. **We are no longer to love the world,**
   "Do not love the world or the things in the world. If anyone loves the world, the love of the father is not in him"1st John 2 v 15.

2. **And also we are no longer to live according to the pattern of this world.**

"Do not conform any longer to the pattern of this world, but be transformed by the renewing of your mind." Romans 12 v 2.

3. **We should not be equally yoked with unbelievers,**

"Do not be yoked together with unbelievers. For what do righteousness and wickedness have in common. Or what fellowship can light have with darkness. What harmony is there between Christ and belial? What does a believer have in common with an unbeliever? What agreement is there between the temple of the living God. As God has said, I will live with them and walk among them, and I will be their God and they will be my people. Therefore come out from them and be separate, says the Lord."

2nd Corinthians 6 v 14.

Because we are Gods children, God wants to dwell in us and walk among us, but He can only do this if we sanctify our lives by living seperate from this world. We cannot live our lives according to the standards of this world and expect God to dwell in us. No way, because friendship with the world is enmity with God.

"Don't you know that friendship with the world is hatred toward God? Anyone who choses to be a friend of the world becomes an enemy of God."

James 4 v 4.

God is an holy God and the world system is fitting to the carnal nature, the adamic nature of sin and not to the holy nature of God. As believers we are to live according to the Spirit and holy nature of God because without holiness no man shall see God.

Also Jesus has called us to be a kingdom and priest to serve God. (Revelation 1 v 6).

God has called us as new testament Levites. In the old testaments, God called the Levites specially unto himself and set them apart to serve in the temple. Although the Levites dwelt among their brothers the Israelites, they were not permitted to live like the Israelite's and could not do as the Israelites were doing. They lived their lives according to set rules, laid down by God himself. They were the only ones permitted to serve and offer sacrifices in the temple of God. They were permitted to enter into the holy place of the temple, while everyone else was restricted to the outer courtyard of the temple of God. However for them to serve and function effectively in their ministerial role, they had to go through a process of pure purification in order to minister officially before God. It is this line of purification that is referred to as living separate from the world.

Please note that although the Levites had automatic qualification into the priesthood ministry, they still had to undergo a purification process.
So it is for Christians. Although the moment we accept Jesus as our Lord and saviour, we automatically qualify as Sons and Daughters of God, but for us to walk in our authority, live up to our full potentials as Son's and Daughter's of the Most High God we have to undergo a

purification process and to do this we must be set apart unto God.

Now symbolically we are not expected to go and live on any high cliff or forest, but we are expected in our hearts and minds to live daily kingdom of God lifestyle and also to always

"Set our minds on things above, not on earthly things."
Colossians 3 v 2.

We are expected to consecrate and dedicate ourselves solely to God and we do this by waiting daily on God, in prayer, fasting, meditation, studying the bible, spending quality time with God alone. We are not expected to mingle with the crowd, because we have been set apart. We are not supposed to do what everyone in the world is doing. We are to be different from the whole world. If the world wanted to see Jesus and know about the kingdom of God, all they had to do was to take a good look at Christians.

Also it does not mean you should not interact with people or go and live in a quiet secluded island. You have to interact because you are not an island and you are still living in this world but your lifestyle should be different.

God has called us to live separated lives, right in the midst of this world not outside this world. We are to be set apart, we are to shine in this dark world, the world is to see us and without a doubt they should know that we are children of God.

(2)

EAGLES ARE VERY ATTENTIVE

Eagles are very attentive, they take time to pay attention and you can never catch them unawares. They are never rattled because they are always alert, watching, waiting, listening and what have you. Eagles are simply superb. As children of God we are expected to be likewise. We have to be very attentive and pay attention to hear from our COMMANDER, THE KING OF KINGS and THE LORD OF HOST.

The prophet Habakkuk said in the book of

Habakkuk 2 v 1 "I will stand my watch and see what God is speaking."

As believers we always have to learn to be still in the presence of God, We have to create that solitary moment or time with God alone and listen out for daily instructions. Friends we live in a very precarious and terrible times that we can't afford not to pay attention. We can't afford to live carelessly.

Proverbs 4 v 20 Says "My son give me your ear/ heart......"

If we do not pay attention we might miss divine instructions. God is committed to leading and guiding us, God is not a silent God, he is a speaking God. But the question or problem is that are we attentive enough to hear him.

"But when he, the Spirit of truth comes, he will guide you into all truth. He will not SPEAK on his own, he will SPEAK only what he hears, and he will TELL you what is yet to come."

John 16 v 13.

In the book of John 10 v 1-5, Jesus said he is the True Shepherd and his sheep LISTEN to his voice. His sheep follow him because they KNOW his voice. Friends you have to develop and train yourself to hear the voice of God. God wants our ears to be fine tuned so that we can be able to hear him.

"You would hear a voice behind you saying this is the way, walk in it"

If you are not attentive you can't hear when God is speaking, because most times God chooses different ways to communicate with us. For instance in the book of 1st Kings v 17 tells about:

When Elijah fled from jezebel, God appeared to him 3 times, the first time he thought God was in the wind, the 2nd time he thought God was in the fire. However

God spoke in a still small voice and Elijah was attentive enough to hear that still small voice.

Also Job gave us another description of how God also speaks, *For God does speak, now one way, now another though man may not perceive it. In a dream, in a vision of the night when deep sleep falls on men as they slumber in their beds, he may speak in their ears and terrify them with warnings, or a man may be chastened on a bed of pain.*
(Job 33 v 14, 19.

So from the above 2 scriptures we can understand 4 ways God can speak to us.

a) Through a still small voice.
b) Through dreams.
c) Through visions.
d) Through trials. God does this to catch our attention. Especially when we get so busy that we fail to seek his face. God used the burning bush to catch the attention of Moses.

God is there to guide us. He is leading us. However, it is the duty of the led to watch out for what the shepherd is saying or which direction, he is leading. If we do not follow his leadings, we might go astray.

The Israelites would not move if the glory cloud did not move. They only moved when it moved. Amen. In every area of our life we are to seek direction. Jesus always retired to solitary places to pray and wait on God.

God kept the Israelites from danger. Eagles see their prey or enemy from afar, even before it comes near.

Life is a warfare, every day the enemy is raging and unleashing fire, but we have an anointing from the Most Holy One, be attentive, follow God's leadings and you would never go astray. Eagles have no time for frivolities. Notwithstanding the length of time Elisha served Elijah, he could not get his request fulfilled by mere talk. He had asked for a double portion of Elijah's anointing. But for him to get it, he had to fulfil a difficult condition, he had to see Elijah when he was to be taken away.

What a tasking condition, it required 100% attention or else it can't be fulfilled. But Elisha was determined and he became very attentive, watching daily, listening daily and observing daily, and alas he saw the chariots of fire taking Elijah away. He got the double portion. This did not come cheap, because we are told he faced some distractions when some of the sons of the prophets who were prophets like himself, came and wanted to distract his attention. However he was so consumed with being attentive that he shut them up.

Friends sometimes you have got to be radical or else there are some folks who do not have the same vision as you have and they would do anything to distract you from where you are going.
Be determined to stay focus and fix your attention only on Jesus, the author and finisher of your faith. Therefore watch, wait, observe and hear what God is saying.

One of the most effective way to hear from God is,

(1) From his word. Lay up his word in your heart and you would never go astray. eg, if you study

his word you do not need to wait and hear a loud voice from heaven. For instance when it comes to borrowing money, you know what the word of God says regarding borrowing, you would therefore restrain yourself and not borrow.

"Thou shall lend and not borrow, because the borrower is a servant to the lender."

Deut 28 v 12

Also if you are tempted to fornicate, the spirit of will bring the word of God regarding fornication straight to your spirit and that would stop you in your tracks.

Also when you study his word you do not need anyone to preach to you about the consequences of Adultery.

Also regarding prosperity, you would learn to pay your tithes, which is 10% of your income. You also would avoid so many silly mistakes.

(3)

EAGLES ARE TENACIOUS, FEARLESS, THEY LOVE THE STORM.

Eagles are never afraid of the storm, no matter how fierce it appears. The Eagle would never turn back or try to hide from the storm. The eagle would rather position itself properly and face the storm squarely by diving right into the face of the storm. Also what the eagle does is that it sees the storm as an opportunity and uses its current to glide into higher altitude. It surfs with the storm, it engages in a roller coaster dimension of flying with the storms. Whoa! what display of wisdom.

Therefore as children of the Most High God we are to model our lives after the pattern of the eagle because we have the seed of an eagle inside of us. GOD IS OUR PAPA EAGLE and we are his CHILDREN EAGLE Therefore we can do all what the eagle does. Please never run from your storms. In life we would face all kinds of storms and storms could be in various form and degree. Storms come in form of challenges such as, financial, loss of job, loss of a loved one, marital breakdown, ill health, unruly children, drug addiction and all sorts.

But through it all, we are more than conquerors. As believers we have to be conscious of the greater one inside of us. 1st John 4 v 4.

God has assured us that he would never leave us nor forsake us. When we pass through the fire it would not consume us. When the storm arises every other bird flies away except the eagle.

The eagle remains resolute in the midst of adversity and remains unperturbed because it has the faith that it can overcome the storms, that is why it dives right into the face, the very eye of the storm.

Friends in this race you have no choice than to build your faith and live by it. "The just shall live by faith."

Let us look at the story of David at his time in Ziglak (1st Sam 30 v 1 - 31). Here was a man anointed to be king, yet he was running for his life from Saul and he lived in caves, just when he thought he had gotten a little respite, then he was attacked, not only that all the people that once rallied around him, now wanted his head off, what was he to do? but he did not allow that to weigh him down, he encouraged himself in the Lord, and got ready to face the storm of oppression and when he did that he fully recovered all.

Also once the eagle finds the direction of the wind of the storm, the eagle stops flapping and uses the pressure of the raging storm to glide into the clouds and soar through it. The eagle does not waste its time trying to investigate where the wind is coming from or starts asking questions or tries to figure out why the storm is blowing in its direction, rather what it does is to reposition itself, and just glides through the storm. It sees the storm as a stepping stone to get to the next level, the next higher dimension of greater heights.

Therefore every child of God is to do same, we have to see challenges as a stepping stone to take us into a higher realm of victory and glory. The eagle believer has to understand that the battle is not his/her own, and should not try to fight the storm, because it is a sheer waste of time and the result would be fruitless, For we wrestle not against flesh and blood, but against spiritual wickedness. The battle is a spiritual battle so you need to fight back spiritually. Do not depend on your strength, but depend on God. For by strength shall no man prevail.

When the eagle wants to face the storm, it stops flapping its wings. It no longer relies on its effort, so we too should not try to use our efforts to overcome our challenges. We are to rely on God to help us overcome. Also do not bother to find out where the storm is coming from. Just know your authority in Christ, and use this authority to quench the storm.

(4)

EAGLES BUILD THIER NEST ON HIGH CLEFTS OF THE ROCK AND IN CRAGS OF MOUNTAIN.

-- As a believer your nest includes your home, finances, relationships, family members, your children, health, and everything that pertains to life and Godliness that surrounds you. You are not to be ignorant of the devices of the devil, who is always looking for opportunity to cause harm and wreck havoc. Therefore you are not to take things for granted. Please leave nothing to chance. Do not dwell on high alone but ensure to include your nest as well with you so that you can keep a close eye on them. Trust God with your kids, finances, your relationships and all the contents of your nest. Your eyes should always be on your nest.

The eyes of the eagle is always watching out for its nest to see if it is being attacked, and once it spots an enemy it swoops down swiftly and quickly prevents the enemy from attacking. The eagle does not wait for the enemy to swoop down on it. It would rather be the first to swoop down on any potential enemy. We have to pray for everything that concerns us. As we dwell on high so should our nest also dwell on high.

Beloved it will surprise you to know that within the body of Christ, most men of God have been very negligent of their nest and this has allowed the devil to prey on their nest easily. The devil has caused so many marriage break up, has caused the children of pastors to go astray, has attacked the finances of pastors, the church and so on. What will you say about this, when a highly annointed minister hears of his wife divorcing him in the news. That is really serious. What went wrong? His wife is supposed to be in his nest, how come the devil was able to penetrate his nest and cause his wife to go to such an extent without his knowledge. We have to be wise and be very vigilant.

Also the eagle goes to great length to ensure its nest is safe and secured, and protected from potential enemies. It does this by,

1. picking up thorns and lays it on the cliff as outer shell of protection and

2. then it brings twigs to form another layer over it for ruggedness and agility.

3. And again it places a layer of thorns over it for the nest to withstand enemies penetration

4. And then places a layer of soft- grass just before the inner most layer of rugs which completes the nest.

5. The finishing touches for the nest is completed with its FEATHERS kept over the outer most layers of rugs.

Beloved, we can see how far the eagle goes to secure it's nest. It does everything to make sure it is well secured, from picking thorns, twigs, more thorns again, soft grass, feathers and above all keeps it's eyes closely on it. Now if we are to analyze the steps one after the other, it will be in this order,

1. Thorns will represent the sword of the spirit, which is the word of God, for the word of God is sharper than any two edged sword. Load your spirit man with the word of God and always prophesy the word of God over your nest.

2. Twigs represent the shield of faith. Faith is tested and made strong through trials and challenges. The winds of adversity will surely blow in the direction of your nest, but you have to stand strong in faith and resist the enemy and the enemy will surely flee.

3. Another layer of thorns, which also represent more swords of the spirit. Always be loaded with the sword of the spirit, so that at any given time, even in the dream YOU CAN BODLY SAY, IT IS WRITTEN. The devil can not stand IT IS WRITTEN, he will surely flee.

4. The layer of soft grass will represent the blood of Jesus. The blood of Jesus seals our final protection in Christ. No demonic power can stand the blood of Jesus. The blood of Jesus broke the back of the devil forever and ever. Secure your nest, by always pleading the blood of Jesus over your nest continuously.

5. Feathers is noted for softness and tenderness and this will represent love, warmth and care. Give your nest the warmth, love and care needed. Do not neglect your nest. Husbands do not neglect your wives, wives do not neglect your husbands, parents do not neglect your children, pastors do not neglect your congregation, etc. The devil was only able to get hold of Eve the moment she was all alone. That was then, however the devil has gone a step further these days that you could be right with your husband and yet he still attacks. Why ? because these days we have a lot of marriages but no union. Therefore it is vital that couples stay in union, by so doing the devil can not penetrate into their midst. Also brood over your nest by praying and meditating over your nest continually.

Therefore you are to go great length to ensure your nest is safe, by fasting, praying and doing all the above.

(5)

EAGLES ENSURE THEIR YOUNG ONES GROW TO BE LIKE THEM.

One key note about eagles is that they see it as a sense of duty to nurture their young ones to grow up to be like them. The eagle does not waver about it, neither does it dilly dally about it. The eagle sees it as a sense of duty and has burden in its heart to see the eaglet grow to become an eagle. This process to an eagle is not optional, it is compulsory.

This is the same way God wants us to see soul winning. Soul winning for every believer should not be optional, but compulsory.

Jesus gave the great commission and commanded in Matthew 28 v 19 that we should go into the world and win souls.

Please to be everything God wants you to be, see soul winning as a burden in your heart.

Also ensure they are well established and rooted in the house of God. The bible says that ... your seed may remain." And whatever you ask the father he would give it to you.

Also those that turn many to righteousness shall shine as the stars of heaven"

We must also nuture them, till they remain rooted. Remember as you sow seeds, the devil is ready to snatch the seed, out of their hearts, so you have to be vigilant in prayer and fasting so that your seed would abide. The mother eagle is very vigilant of her young, and would nuture them until they are able to stand on their own and soar high like themselves.

(6)

EAGLES ARE GOOD STOCK KEEPERS

"Examine yourself to see if you are still standing in the faith."
2nd Corinthians 13 v 5.

You have to from time to time take stock to see whether you are still standing in the faith. The bible says let him that stands take heed, lest he falls. The eagle is a very peculiar bird, it does not leave anything to chance. When an eagle gets to a certain age, it notices that it's perfomance is deterioting or not according to standard, it quietly retreats to a mountaintop. On the mountain top, it settles down over a five month period of time. It knocks off its own beak by banging it against a rock, this causes bleeding and it is very painful, but the eagle endures this painful process and it plucks out its talons, then feathers until it is completely bare.

At this stage the eagle is stripped of everything and now relies solely on nature to take it's course. God wants us to rely absolutely on him, we have to strip ourselves bare before his presence. We have to be empty. God will only fill empty vessels. The eagle will then wait untill all new feathers and beak grows back. This process revitalises the eagle and enables it to fly once again dynamically and royally without much effort or toil. When God fills us up, we would fly in a supernatural dimension.

To get the best of God you have to be broken. You have to empty self out, so that God can fill you up. You have to submit and totally surrender to the Lordship of Jesus Christ. Your will must be swallowed up in his will. You have to learn to lay it all down at the foot of the cross and allow the cross to re- mold you. Look at the eagle, it lays it all down on the mountain. Remember when it does that it becomes absolutely helpless, selfless, all its strength is gone, no more feathers and now it relies 100% on its maker to re mold it and make it to become a better eagle.

Beloved to be greatly used by God and to become a vessel of honour in the hands of God you have to take a cue from the eagle. Do what it does and in no time you will be soaring high on the heights of glory. Learn to purge yourself from time to time, don't think you have arrived. Learn to hide under the blood and always yearn to enclose yourself under the everlasting arms of God.
He that dwells under the shadow of the most high shall abide under the shadow of the Almighty.

Ps 91 v 1.

Likewise from time to time, we have to make sure our old man is crucified and remains crucified forever. We soar very high when the old man is done away with, because God is a spirit and we his worshippers must worship him in truth and spirit. The flesh is enmity with God. We can't with the carnal nature contact God, because God is a spirit. Amen. DO NOT THINK YOU KNOW IT ALL OR YOU HAVE ARRIVED. TAKE TIME TO SEEK GOD AND DEPEND ON HIM TO PRUNE YOU, TO TAKE AWAY PRIDE.

Jesus while here on earth at intervals always withdrew to solitary places to pray and be alone with God. Ps 103 v 5. Isa 40 v 31

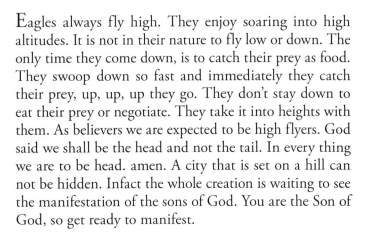

(7)

EAGLES ARE HIGH FLYERS.

"Who are these that fly along like clouds, like doves to their nest."

Isaiah 60 v 8.

Eagles always fly high. They enjoy soaring into high altitudes. It is not in their nature to fly low or down. The only time they come down, is to catch their prey as food. They swoop down so fast and immediately they catch their prey, up, up, up they go. They don't stay down to eat their prey or negotiate. They take it into heights with them. As believers we are expected to be high flyers. God said we shall be the head and not the tail. In every thing we are to be head. amen. A city that is set on a hill can not be hidden. Infact the whole creation is waiting to see the manifestation of the sons of God. You are the Son of God, so get ready to manifest.

We are children of God, children of light. Our light has to shine for all men to see. We are a royal priesthood, a chosen generatinon, a holy nation, a people called to show case the glory of God. We are peculiar. Like the eagle which is a peculiar bird. We are a rare gem. So if we are not shinning there is something wrong somewhere. In the old testament a whole nation was afraid of Isaac, he was richer than a whole nation, and they had to drive him away. Abraham had his own trained soldiers and he defeated 3 great kings. Amen. Daniel ruled with 3 kings. Joseph was made prime minister in a foriegn land. King nebudcadnezeer bowed down to daniel and his friends.

The nation of Israel baffled kings, nations and is still doing the same today. Imagine Israel is a very small nation in the middle east, yet no nation can prevail against them. Why? because the covenant is still speaking.

Eagles do not grumble on the ground with pigeons. They do not murmur. No. Not at all. Or negotiate with unbelievers or the world. Infact they do not live like the world does. Their mind is set on the kingdom of God. They are kingdom minded and focused. They have an understanding of the times. An eagles focus is always upward. Eagles most often than not never look down, the only time they do look down is to catch their prey and this is done pretty swiftly after that up, up they go. God said he would set us up on high, above all nations, peoples and kings shall come to the brightness of our light.

The whole world paid homage to king Solomon and came to learn wisdom at his feet. Whoa, what a mighty God we serve.
All the kings of the earth sought audience with Solomon to hear the wisdom God had put in his heart. Year after year everyone who came brought a gift.
2nd Chronicles 9 v 23.

God has designed you to be an eternal excellence, to show forth his glory. Nations will come to your light and kings to the brightness of your dawn. Isaiah 60 v 3.

Eagle believers are trail blazers. Eagles display an exceptional high acumen of wisdom. Therefore as an eagle Christian you can display a high level of wisdom, for witty inventions, breakthrough in scientific research and all sorts because you have the mind of Christ.

Also God's power in you radiates and flows out to everyone you come into contact with.

God worked extra-ordinary miracles through the hands of Paul. Handkerchiefs from his body healed the sick. The shadow of Peter raised healed the sick. The apostles raised the dead, delivered the oppressed. etc.

(8)

EAGLES DO NOT EAT DEAD PREY

... Daily they source for food. We are to wait on God every day. We are to study our bibles, pray, meditate, praise God. Christianity is a daily affair. Vultures eat dead prey. Anything goes. Vultures get carried away with every wind of doctrine. False doctrine etc. An eagle would not. Because an eagle waits on the Lord daily, he is able to know which is which, he can't be swept away by false doctrine. Everything of the world is dead, things of this world causes death, death to the spirit man, seperation from God. We are to feed on the word of life, the incorruptible word which is able to make us. We are to fix his word in our heart and soul. (Duet 11 v 18)

Eagles watch what they eat. They are careful what they take in. Whatever they can't digest they would not eat. They do not feed on pornography, scrap, satanic news, books, slander, jokes, dirty words via phone, text messaging. When you do such stuff you are eating dead stuff. Anything that is worldly based or attached to this world is dead prey. Friendship with the world is enmity with God and death. Feed on living things, The word of God is living and active.

The word of God is life. Feed on the word daily. Jesus is the living Word. His flesh is food, whosoever feeds on me would never die. Soak your self in the word. Eat his word daily, by studying your bible, feed your spirit man with fresh manna from the throne room of God. Meditate, study, digest, ponder on the word. Vultures and hyenas feed on dead carcass. Anything attached to this world is death. Vultures over eat and get intoxicated, such that they can't fly or move and thus become prey for other animals. To be an eagle believer watch what you take in through your three senses. And there are three gates/channels through which we take things in;

(1) EYES GATE.
-What are you feeding your eyes with.

(2) THE EARS GATE. - What are you listening to.

(3) MOUTH GATE.
- What are you saying. Jesus said in Matthew 15 v 11 that it is not what you take in that defiles a man, but what comes out of your mouth that defiles a man. Out of the abundance of the heart the mouth speaks.

Speak right words. How forcible are right words. Shapen your life with right words.

⊚⊚⊚⊚⊚

(9)

EAGLES ARE FAITHFUL LOVERS

Eagles stick to one partner all their entire lifetime. Once they get hooked up, that is the end of the matter and they stay forever faithful to each other in their lifetime. Likewise we are also expected to stay faithful to God. God loves and rewards faithfulness. We have to stay faithful and true to God. The major problem God had with the children of Israelites was that they never stayed faithful to God, they always went after other gods. God does not like spiritual prostitutes.

Spiritual prostitutes are those who have other lovers (gods) aside from God. God is a jealous God and we are God's bride. We are expected to remain faithful to God.

Friends, if you remain faithful to God, he would make your feet like hinds feet and you would ride on the high places of this world." Habakkuk 3 v 19.

In this walk of faith just like the eagle clings to its partner for life, we are to do likewise. We are to put our hands on the plough and never look back. We are to hook up to Jesus the lover of our soul and walk together with him forever. We are to walk with God in faith because THE JUST SHALL LIVE BY FAITH. Only God is to be our praise, our love. The greatest of all the commandments admonishes us to love the Lord our God with all our heart, with all our soul and mind.

Matthew 22 v 37.

(10)

EAGLES HAVE EXCELLENT VISION.

Son of man, I have made you a watchman for the house of Israel, so hear the word I speak.

Ezekiel 33 v 7.

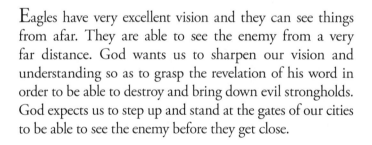

Eagles have very excellent vision and they can see things from afar. They are able to see the enemy from a very far distance. God wants us to sharpen our vision and understanding so as to grasp the revelation of his word in order to be able to destroy and bring down evil strongholds. God expects us to step up and stand at the gates of our cities to be able to see the enemy before they get close.

We are to be on top of our game, the enemy should never take us by surprise. It is very ungodly for that to happen, because God has given us dominion and authority over all the powers of darkness. We have the authority to trample upon the enemy, and you trample only on things that are beneath you, under your feet, therefore if the enemy takes you by surprise and defeats you, then that means the enemy has been able to crawl from under your feet, then climb up to your knee, then to your shoulders and finally to your head. Oh dear! What were you looking at? We are to stand our watch so as to enable us to put the enemy permanently where it belongs, that is under our feet. But to do so you have to be vigilant and be always on the watch.

Also to survive in these last days, you must be a step ahead, you must be abreast and have knowledge of things before they occur. To do this you need the Holy Spirit, because the bible says the Holy Spirit would tell us of things to come.

God revealed to Elisha the plans of the 2nd Kings 6 v 8-11. Friends we are in the last days and the bible says in the Last days I would pour out my spirit on all flesh, and your young men shall see vision. These are the last days. The days of his spirit. As an eagle believer you must crave for the infilling of the power of God. You need the Holy Spirit. Without the Holy Spirit you can do nothing. You can't function as a Christian, Hence every believer should have a relationship with the Holy Spirit.

He is our Helper. He reveals secrets to us. Elisha, knew what the king was discussing in his bedroom. The Holy Spirit would give you vision spiritually, he would lead you the way you should go etc.

If you are a believer nothing should hit you suddenly. God can't do anything without not telling his servants and also the Holy Spirit would reveal any plan of the enemy to you. Amos 3 v 7

The strong vision of the eagle keeps the enemy away from its nest, because it can sight the enemy from afar and deals with it before it comes close.

(11)

EAGLES ENDURE TESTING.

GOD WILL TEST US.

The female eagle test the male eagle before trusting. But the male eagle endures it. The female eagle goes to a certain height and throws a twig for the male to catch. Once the male catches hold of it and brings it back, the female flies into a higher altitude and drops it again.

This is repeated over and over again until the female has assurance that the male has mastered the art of seriously picking up the twigs in love. Once the male and female gets hooked up in trust they stick together for life. Similarly God will test us as well. Our faith will be tested and tried. 1st peter 4 v 12, psalm 34 v 19, deut 32 v 11, deut 33 v 26. God tested the Israelites.

God will test us to see if we will be faithful to him, God loves faithfulness.

God also put Abraham to test and Abraham passed all the test. And God was pleased with Abraham and had confidence in him.

Can God trust you that you would remain faithful to him?

(12)

EAGLES HAVE A CLEAR UNDERSTANDING OF "VISION, PLAN AND PURPOSE."

One of the distinctive features of an eagle, is that it understands VISION, PLAN AND PURPOSE. The eagle understands the vision for its life, understands the plan why it was created distinct from other birds and goes ahead to fulfil its purpose as an eagle and not as an ordinary bird.

Therefore as children of God, we have God as our father eagle so we are meant to follow suit and have a clear understanding of VISION, PLAN AND PURPOSE of God for our lives.

Every eaglet is born with a vision, plan and purpose. But the eaglet can not unleash this potential embedded inside it, on its own. It needs to identify, know and associate with the parent eagle to be able to birth out what is deposited inside of it.

This same contrast applies to children of God, the moment we accept Jesus as our Lord and personal saviour, there is a switch of kingdoms and with our new birth God deposits great potentials inside of us. We now belong to God and God becomes our father. We are now new creatures in Christ Jesus. (2nd Corinthians 5 v 17).

However to unleash this wonderful potentials inside of us, we need to go a step further to associate and have a closer relationship with God.

Now because the eagle is a bird that understands vision, plan and purpose, it ensures that it helps the eaglet to grasp this understanding as well, so that the eaglet can fulfil destiny by becoming an eagle.

Likewise God does not want us to remain the same as we were at new birth, but he wants us to grow in faith;

"Until we all reach unity in the faith and in the knowledge of the Son of God and become mature attaining to the whole measure of the fullness of Christ. Then we will no longer be infants tossed back and forth."
Ephesians 3 v 13 - 14.

It is pertinent to note that the eagle takes this phase very seriously, because without it doing so, the eaglet would remain in its nest and would refuse to fly. The eaglet is not destined or created to remain in a nest. So, to be able to make the eaglet fulfil destiny and finally become an eagle, the eagle subjects the eaglets to rigorous training, by teaching the eaglets to fly.

Likewise our heavenly father would also subject us to training, so that we can attain full maturity in Christ and begin to walk as Jesus walked while here on earth, do the miracles Jesus did and even fulfil this scripture which says;

"Greater works than these (Christ did) shall you do also.
"John 14 v 12.

To grow into Christ image does not come cheap. We have to submit ourselves to be trained. We have to undergo God's boot camp, we must go through the wilderness experience. There is no short cut into Canaan. The only way into Canaan is the wilderness. When the children of God left Egypt, God made them to go through the wilderness, because he wanted to teach them his ways, reveal himself to them, and have a very close relationship with them, before releasing them into their destination, which is Canaan. God also wanted them to be fortified and rooted in him, so that when they got into Canaan, they would be able to stand and remain strong, they would be able to distinguish between wrong and evil and would not adopt the ways of the land they were going to posses.

Also God wanted them to have different ideology from what they had in Egypt. God wanted them to break away from their old mediocre ways of thinking and to think according to their new way of life, the kingdom style. Likewise God wants every child of his, to break away from the nest, break away from the old way of living, from the old line of thoughts and come along with him to experience the abundant life he has given us.

God has so much in store for us and as long us we refuse to come out from our nest, we can not grasp the things God has prepared for us.

"Eyes have not seen, no ears has heard, no mind has conceived what God has prepared for those who love him." 1st Corinthians 2 v 9.

Abraham was an example, despite the promises God made to him, he was still thinking according to his old mediocre way in regards to the law of succession. In those days anyone who died without an heir to his estate, would automatically have a servant in his household inherit him. That was the norm and the acceptable way of inheritance, back then.

And we can see this in Genesis 15 v 1;

"But Abraham said, O Sovereign Lord, what can you give me since I remain childless and the one who will inherit my estate is Eliezer of Damascus. And Abraham said, you have given me no children, so a servant in my household will be my heir.

I am sure God had a big laugh at what Abraham said, because God simply ordered Abraham to come out of his tent, out of his nest, out of his old way of thinking and God told him to look up at the heavens and see the bigger picture God had for him. God had bigger and a larger than life plan for Abraham's life and as long as Abraham remained in his tent, he could never see it nor understand it. Likewise, God is calling someone today, right now, to come out of their shallow thinking and think big, think according to the magnitude of the bigness of God and not according to the frailty of your challenges. For your challenges are nothing compared to our God.

"Then he took him outside and said, Look up at the heavens and count the stars, if indeed you can count them. Then he said so shall your offspring be."

Genesis 15 v 5.

God wants us to see into the broader perspective of his purpose, vision and plan for our lives. Beginning from the moment Abraham came out of his tent/nest and saw what God showed him, he broke away from his mediocre thinking and hooked up to a new realm of thoughts and he was able to grasp the entire vision, plan and purpose of God for his life and began soaring with it.

"Abram believed the Lord, and he credited it to him as righteousness."

Genesis 15 v 6.

Friends, as long as you remain in your nest, you can not walk in the supernatural.

It is as simple as that because the nest represents the worlds system. You can't confine yourself to the world and it's system and expect to flow in the supernatural power of God.

Now back to mother eagle, when the mother eagle sees that time has come for the eaglet to learn how to fly, she gathers the eaglet on its back and spreading her wings flies high. Suddenly she swoops out from under the eaglet and allows the eaglet to fall, as the eaglet falls it gradually learns what it wings are meant for, and swiftly the mother eagle catches it again.

Similarly God does the same for us, as we undergo training. And this can be seen in;
Exodus 19 v 4 "I bore you on eagles wings."

The above scripture gives us a beautiful and inspiring picture of how God trains us. The word bore means to lift by divine power. We should never think myopically for a fraction of a second that God is far off and allowing us to undergo through trials alone. No God is not, as a matter of fact he bears us on his wings, just as the mother eagle does.

And God has assured us in his word that he would never leave us nor forsake us.

Also in Psalm 46 v 1 God is an ever present help in trouble.

God is right there with you, through the fire, God is there and the fire will not burn you, through the waters he is there, that is why the waters will not drown you. (Isaiah 43 v 2).

God will allow us to go through the storm, so as to train us so that we can not only fly but also to soar high. We have to leave the elementary things of christianity and move unto the maturity stage.

"Therefore let us leave the elementary teaching about Christ and go on to maturity, not laying again the foundation of repentance from acts that lead to death." Heb 6 v 1.

During training we imbibe the attributes of what makes PAPA eagle soar high. All that Christ are, we are to become. Christ is our Eagle father, so we have to allow him to train us and teach us how to fly high like he did while he was here on earth. On earth Jesus performed many signs and wonders and Jesus said in John 14 v 12 that we are to do greater works than he did. But we can only do greater works if we yield ourselves to be trained. WE MUST ALLOW GOD TO TRAIN US.

Now back to mother eagle. Mother eagle does not expect the eaglet to fly at the first attempt, so it patiently repeats this same line of procedure, but with different strategies and approach until it is satisfied that the eaglet is ready to fly.

Likewise, God would allow us to go through trials and testing, this is for our own good so as to make us tenacious, consistent, patient, strong and build us up to become rooted in our faith. When persecutions come your way, remember God is teaching you how to fly, Also the eaglet does not learn how to fly at the first attempt until after it is being thrown down severally before it learns how to flutter it's wings until it realizes it can fly. Similarly we also go through several series of trials just to build us up and make us unshakable.

Also God will test us to see, whether we will trust in him fully, whether we will stand firm in our faith, and whether we will hold unto him always. God himself does the teaching, although he uses human vessels to achieve this sometimes.

However know for sure that after you have endured the wilderness process, you would come out victorious. Remember not to grumble during trials and persecutions, for we are learning how to fly.

Gold in its original form looks very crude, undesirable, black and crusty. But after it has gone through the refiners fire, it comes out shinning, beautiful, adorable, precious, worthy, glittering such that everyone takes notice of it.

However before the gold got to its final stage of glitter and admiration, it went through various painful processes of refining and refining.

When he has tested me, I will come forth as gold.
Job 23 v 10.

Friends, your process of refining would surely come with pain, uneasiness, discomfort but you have to hold on and endure, for in the end you would come out as fine gold and everyone would admire you. And "Nations shall come to your light, and kings to the brightness of your dawn." (Isaiah 60 v 3).

Stirring the nest.

Now after all that training, the mother eagle expects the eaglet to fly on its own. But if it sees that the young eaglet is slow to learn or still refuses to fly, it returns the eaglet back to its nest. And this time around it adopts a final procedure. And this is stirring up the nest. It does this because it knows that;

1. The eaglet is not destined to remain in the nest.

2. The eaglet is becoming too attached to the nest such as the same old way of thinking, same old way of doing things, same ideas] and the eaglet is refusing to think big.

3. The eaglet is meant to be cruising in a very high altitude, in the realm of the skies and not sitting crouched up in the nest.

4. The eaglet loves the comfort zone and needs a kick on the backside to move to the next level.

Now the eagle starts stirring the nest, by tearing it apart, [I am sure the eagle would be muttering these words in the process, you are too holed in here, come on, move ahead, get out of here, you are not meant to be here, come fly along with me].

"Like an eagle stirs up its nest and hoovers over it young, then it spreads it's wings to catch them and carries them on its pinions, so the Lord alone led them."
Deuteronomy 32 v 11 - 14.

Likewise God will stir our nest so we do not cling to stuff that will limit us, we have to let go of pride, let go of malice, let go of being judgemental, let go off self, let go of besetting sins, put off any hindrance and come along with him to experience the higher life, a new way of living he has called us into.

Now after the nest is torn apart and destroyed,

1). The eaglet realises that there is nothing to cling to and that it needs help urgently and desperately. The eaglets frantically searches for mother eagle. Friends if we get to this stage of desperation in our search for God, we would definitely find him. If we search for God as a deer PANTS after water, we will find him.
And God confirms this in
Jeremiah 29 v 13 *"Then you will seek me, inquire for and require me [as a vital necessity] and find me with all your heart, I will be found by you."*

"But if from there, you seek the Lord your God, you will find him, If you look for him with all your heart and with all your soul." Deuteronomy 4 v 29.

2). The eaglet needs help and it has now come to this understanding that help can only come from mother eagle, therefore it does not look down, nor sideways, but it focuses its gaze upward towards mother eagle. Therefore as children of God we must understand that help, comes from nowhere but God alone. The Psalmist says in Psalm 121 v 1
"I will lift up my eyes to the hills, where does my help come from. My help comes from the Lord, the maker of heaven and earth."

3). Finally the eaglet reaches out towards the mother eagle. At this stage the eaglet, abandons its will, its desires, breaks away from its nest environment and finally surrenders to do the will of mother eagle, which is to fly. This is a defining moment because it is the eaglet breaking away, dropping all its personal ambition and saying mother eagle, here I come to do your will and not my will anymore. It is in the midst of this surrender, that PURPOSE, VISION and DESTINY is birthed because the eaglet has become an eagle.

4). Now the eaglet flutters its wings and begins to fly higher and higher. It begins to glide and soar in the wide open sky. Finally the eaglet is now an eagle, strong, matured and able to deal with the storms and torrents. Similarly that is how, God expects us to be, strong and matured in our faith, able to distinguish between good and evil, able to deal with challenges and overcome trials. Because through it all, we are more than conquerors.

Friends just as the eaglet surrendered to the mother eagle and finally became an eagle, so must we surrender and yield ourselves to God. Until we yield to God's will, we would continue struggling. God can only use yielded vessels and the moment we yield to his will, we would automatically see ourselves flying. This is an awakening, it is time to leave the elementary teachings of Christ and go on to maturity so we can not only fly, but also to soar high and above into the realms of glory.

෧෧෧෧෧

(13)

EAGLES KNOW WHEN IT IS TIME TO DIE. THEY DO NOT DIE CARELESLLY THEY DIE GLORIOUSLY.

With long life will I satisfy you.

Ps 91 v 16

One of the covenant right we have as believers is long life. When it is time for the eagle to die it flies to the highest of mountains, lies down and looks straight into the sun and passes on. What a glorious way to die. The eagle just lies down, unperturbed until it dies naturally. The eagle does not fall prey to any animal, nor does it die carelessly. It dies gloriously.

In Gen 49 v 33, when it was time for Jacob to die this was how he went about it,
After he had finished giving instructions to his sons, he drew his feet up into the bed, breathed his last and was gathered to his people." Amen.

As an eagle believer, you are not expected to die carelessly. No way. Because the bible says God would give his angels charge over you. Angels would guard you wherever you go. Also God himself would be your shield. He (that is you) that dwells in the secret place of the Most High, shall abide under the shadow of the almighty. (Psalm 91 v 1)

God is your protector. God was as a pillar of cloud to the Israelites in the day time and at night as a pillar of fire. Beloved I will encourage you to read and confess Psalm 91 daily.

Also God gave Moses notice of his death. Moses and Aaron knew when they were both going to die. Abraham, Elisha and most of the patriachs in the old testament also had foreknowledge of their deaths. None of them died by accident. Child of God, accidental and careless death is not meant for you. God is not pleased with the death of the unsaved, how much more you as his child. Friends God eyes are always on you, to protect you and deliver you from evil. God is too faithful.

Also there were two notable people in the bible that God did not allow to witness death physically, God actually took them straight away with him into heaven. These were Enoch in Genesis 5 v 24 and Elijah in 2nd kings 2 v 11. They never witnessed death.

Also in Philippians 1 v 22, Apostle Paul was always calling the shots, when it came to death. He was deciding the right time to die. He was here and there, at a time he said he would stay on earth a little longer because of his disciples. Amen. What a good God we serve. Salvation is beautiful.

(14)

EAGLES DO NOT FLY, THEY SOAR.

But those who hope in the Lord, will renew their strength. They will soar on wings like eagles.

Isaiah 40 v 31.

Birds fly. But only eagles soar. What does it mean to soar. To soar means to ride on the winds effortlessly. The eagle observes the direction of the wind and then flows into it. The eagle does not use its effort when it is soaring, it does not flap its wings, it just mounts on the currents of the wind and the wind pushes it to soar and glide into greater heights.

You use less effort when you soar. As a child of God, with your own effort you can't go far. You need the power of God to soar high. You need the wind of the Holy Spirit to take you into greater heights. You need God's presence all around you. The presence of God will take you to great heights. When you carry Gods presence, situations would bow, problems will disappear, mountains would crumble at God's presence.

Imagine the speed of an aircraft to that of a vehicle, or even the speed of a space rocket to an aircraft and an automobile to a bicycle. The difference is absolutely incomprehensible. When you fly you flap your wings and before long you would get tired, but when you soar you do not use your effort, God carries you and he would take you to greater heights. Amen.

(15)

EAGLES ARE NOTED FOR THEIR EXCEPTIONAL STRENGTH.

Eagles exhibit such an amazing strength that can't be understood. Eagles can carry animals twice as much as its weight. For instance if an eagle weighs 20kg, it can carry an animal that weighs 40 kg. Is this not stunning, how possible could that be, bearing in mind that the eagle always catches its prey alive and then carries it to the highest of mountains.

Well, we serve a God who does amazing things. God does incredible things, things that the human mind can't comprehend.

As children of God we have been endowed to exhibit such unique strength as well. However we are not expected to go and carry heavy objects, but we are mandated to do things and achieve great exploits that ordinarily no one can do or achieve with their own strength, for by strength shall no man prevail. We are simply for signs and wonders.

We are to do exceptional things that naturally looks impossible, things we can't achieve or do in our strength.

"Even youths grow tired and weary, and young men stumble and fall, but those who hope in the Lord will renew their strength. They will soar on wings like eagles, they will run and not grow weary, they will walk and not be faint."
Isaiah 40 v 30-31.

Also we have an anointing from the holy one, after the order of Samson and David. There is a spirit in man and the Holy Spirit empowers us and makes us attain great and unimaginable heights. Amen.

(16)

EAGLES PREPARE THEMSELVES

DAILY.

I will stand my watch and station myself on the ramparts, I will look to see what he will say to me.
Habakkuk 2 v 1.

Because of their flight the previous day, every morning the eagle runs through its feathers, make sure it is in order, and prepares itself for the day. After getting all things in place, the eagle launches out for the day. As an eagle Christian you must not start the day, without praying and worshiping the king of kings, your heavenly father. You must start your day with Jesus Christ and run through the word of God. Commit the day into God's hands before stepping out of your house every day.

Also the eagle would not launch out for the day, until it is sure that everything such as its wings, feathers, beak, claws etc is in order. Hence as eagle Christian's we have to make sure we are in right standing with God and everything including our Christian faith and relationship with people is in order, because the trumpet can sound at anytime.

We have to make sure we are ever ready for the sound of the trumpet, because no one knows the hour and time Jesus would come. Therefore take a cue from the eagle and ;

"Be dressed ready for service and keep your lamps burning, like men waiting for their master to return from a wedding banquet, so that when he comes and knocks they can immediately open the door for him"
Luke 12 v 35-36.

BOOK THREE

70 THINGS GOD HATES

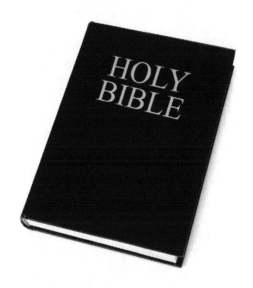

JEMIMA ALARA

Introduction

"Thy word have I hidden in my heart that I should not sin against thee."

Psalm 119 v 11.

God referred to King David as a man after his heart. David pursued after God with all his heart and his soul and his desire was for God all through his lifetime. Also he sought to please God and for him to be able to do this successfully, he held on to the commandments of God very dearly and he was able to abide by them because he kept the commandments close to his heart.

The desire of every true child of God must be to please God and in order to do so, we must not be oblivious of God's commandments but must be able to know what God hates and we would try very hard to avoid doing the things he hates. But you need to know what he hates and this is what part 3 of this book is all about.

Furthermore we are in the last days and these are very precarious times. The forces of darkness through the world system are trying very hard and doing everything they know to try to erase the knowledge of God. They are using government institutions and bodies to make ungodly laws and telling us wrong is right and right is wrong. This is becoming alarming, because even godly parents are losing focus and are not even teaching the younger generation about God. And we are gradually seeing this scripture Judges 2 v 10 coming to pass.

'After that whole generation had been gathered to their fathers, another generation grew up. Who knew neither the Lord nor what he had done for Israel."

As a result of the older generation, not teaching the younger generation about God, this has left the younger generation to become vulnerable and they now look up to society to tell them what to do. Society is teaching our younger ones how to be tolerant and to accept abnormality as normal and wrong as right. Society is teaching our younger people that it is normal and acceptable to be a gay, hetrosexual, bisexual, a lesbian, and even a transgender.

Please parents, older generation arise and teach the younger ones the laws and commandments of God. If you don't, society will twist the truth for them. Society is telling our young ones, it is acceptable to undergo sex change. What, this is so outrageous and appalling. The bible says we are all fearfully and wonderfully made, God in his own wisdom formed a male child right from inception in the womb as a male child yet society says it is alright to change that status and undergo a sex change to become a woman. Friends no matter how many surgeries a male undergoes, he can never be a woman. Can a man carry a baby for 9 months in the tummy and go through labor like a woman and give birth. Can a man have monthly periods, can a man breastfeed a baby? God is greater than man,

Whatever God does is forever, (if he has formed a male child, forever it will be a male, likewise if he has formed a female child forever it will be a female.) nothing can be added to it and nothing can be taken from it. God does it so that men will revere him.

Eccles 3 v 14.

We mortals have to fear God. Enough of all this societal and jet age rubbish.

The truth is the truth, and the truth is God's commandment is against homosexuality and God does not stand for it, neither does he tolerate homosexual acts. The fact that society and the worldly system say it is alright and even government bodies pass laws to legalise gay marriage and union does not make it right. What is right is the word of God. Also the fact that society accepts tattoo as trendy and fashionable, does not make it right. The word of God is clear in Leviticus 19 v 28b, it says "Do not put tattoo marks on yourself."

The world must not tell Christians how to live, rather we Christians should tell the world how to live godly lives that is pleasing to God.

However I know there is a remnant, who would say no to what society is calling right, that we know is wrong. A remnant who would go according to the commandments of God and would not deviate from it, a remnant who would proudly beat their chest and say,

"The lord is our Judge, the Lord is our lawgiver, the Lord is our king, it is he who will save us."

Isaiah 33 v 22.

Over the next few pages, we shall be looking at 70 things God hates and these are all found in the holy scriptures, the greatest constitution that never fails and abides forever.

There are definitely more, but so far this is what God has laid in my heart and I encourage you to study the bible more and as you do so, the almighty God himself will open your eyes and teach you more.

REMAIN BLESSED.

God Hates

---

(1)
IDOLATORY.

"You shall have no other gods before me. You shall not make for yourself an idol in the form of anything in heaven above or on the earth beneath or in the waters below. You shall not bow down to them, for I the Lord your God am a jealous God."

Exodus 20 v 3-5.

This can be broken into 5 different categories.

We have,

1) **Rituals and sacrifices.** Worshipping God in a way that involves the use of rituals and offering sacrifices in the form of slaughtering animals, such as goats, fowls, pigeons and so on. Jesus has paid the ultimate sacrifice with his blood, hence no other sacrifice is required.

"But now Christ has appeared once for all at the end of the ages to do away with sin by the sacrifice of himself."

Hebrew 9 v 26b.

There are some religion that demands that animal sacrifices be made for the atonement of sin and to appease God. Please that is pure idolatry. Jesus is the end of all sacrifices and through him and only by Jesus can our sins be forgiven.

Also there are some countries where they claim to worship God by consulting oracles, visiting local shrines, and engaging in divination. Please we are to refrain from such practices, because God does not exist in local shrines made by man, nor can God be consulted through demonic means called oracles. This is purely a demonic practice and amounts idolatry.

2) **Immortalized beings.** Worshipping God through immortalized human beings, such as Ghandi, Buddha, etc. Also making intercessions to God through Mary the Mother of Jesus can be classified as idolatry. The bible is clear on this issue. Jesus is the only way to the father, there is no other way.

Jesus answered, I am the way and the truth and the life. No one comes to the father except through me.

John 14 v 6.

There is nothing bad to honour Mary the mother of Jesus, because the bible admonishes us to give honour to whom honour is due, but going beyond that and using her as an intermediary to intercede to God on ones behalf is purely classified as idolatry. Jesus is and forever will be the only intermediary for anyone to have access to God.

3) **Graven Images.** Making graven images and worshipping them is idolatry. Most people engage in this practice and the bible warns that no one should engage in such practice.

> *"Do not become corrupt and make yourselves an idol, an image of any shape whether formed like a man or a woman or like any animal on earth or any bird that flies in the air, or like any creature that moves along the ground or any fish in the waters below."*
> *Deuteronomy 4 v 16.*

Also do not worship man-made gods of wood and stone, which can't see or hear or eat or smell.

4) **False worship.** Also worshipping God by bowing down to the Sun, Moon, stars is classified as idolatry.

> *"And when you look up to the sky and see the sun, the moon and the stars all the heavenly array do not be enticed into bowing down to*

them and worshipping things the Lord your God has apportioned to all the nations under heaven."

Deuteronomy 4 v 19.

5) **Self Idolatory.** Anything you put first or prioritise first over God can be classified as idolatry.

Love the Lord your God with all your heart and with all your soul and with all your mind.

Matthew 22 v 37.

Also anything that you allow to take the place of God in your heart is idolatry. This particular aspect is very subtle and most people especially born again Christians are guilty of it without knowing so.

a) For instance if you buy a new car and you put the car first before God, that car automatically becomes an idol.

b) Also if you marry a wife or a husband and your wife or husband takes the place of your heart before God, that husband or wife automatically becomes an object of idolatry. We are commanded to love the Lord our God with all our heart and soul and mind. You are to love your spouse, but not at the detriment of your relationship with God. For instance swapping your quiet time with God and preferring to spend it with your spouse. As time goes on your love for God would grow cold. Subtle way of idolatry. This happened to King Solomon, because he loved foreign women and in no time they turned his heart away from the Lord into idolatry.

c) Also putting your confidence or faith in any other thing apart from God is classified as idolatry. If you put your confidence in your money, career, ability, job, your boss at work, all constitutes idolatry. Choosing to do extra hours at work rather than go for bible studies is idolatry, because the extra money means more to you than your fellowship with God.

(2)

GOD FROWNS WHEN WE LOVE THE WORLD.

"Don't you know that friendship with the world is hatred toward God. Anyone who chooses to be a friend of the world becomes an enemy of God."

James 4 v 4.

"Do not love the world or anything in the world. If anyone loves the world the love of the father is not in him. For everything in the world, the cravings of sinful man, the lust of the eyes and the boasting of what he has and does, comes not from the father but from the world."

1st John 2 v 15.

"For the whole world is under the control of the evil one."

1st John 5 v 19.

(3)

GOD HATES PRIDE.

"God resists the proud, but gives grace to the humble."

James 4 v 6.

"Whoever has haughty eyes and a proud heart, him will I not endure."

Psalm 101 v 5b.

"I hate pride and arrogance."

Proverbs 8 v 13b.

"God detest all the proud of heart, be sure of this they will not go unpunished."

Proverbs 16 v 5.

(4)

GOD HATES ROBBERY AND INIQUITY.

"For I the Lord love justice, I hate ROBBERY AND INIQUITY."

Isaiah 61 v 8.

God has spoken and he has made his mind known to us in the above scripture. God has said he hates robbery and iniquity. We would look at the first one which is robbery.

ROBBERY--In the kingdom of God robbery is when you do not pay your tithes and offerings to God.

"But you ask, how are we to return, will a man rob God.? Yet you rob me. You ask, how do we rob you? In tithes and offerings. You are under a curse- the whole nation of you, because you are robbing me."

Malachi 3 v 8-9.

God commands us to pay our tithes. Tithes is 1/10 of all our earnings and they belong to God, not us.

"A tithe of everything from the land, whether grain from the soil or fruit from the trees belong to God it is holy to the Lord."
Leviticus 27 v 30.

INIQUITY.

Iniquity is an unrepentant heart. A heart that refuses to repent. When you keep sinning and sinning and refuse to repent gradually you would feel very comfortable committing that sin, at this stage that sin becomes iniquity. God hates an unrepentant heart.

(5)

GOD HATES THE DEEDS OF FAITHLESS MEN.

"The deeds of faithless men I hate, they will not cling to me."

Psalm 101 v 3b.

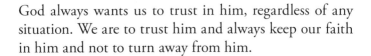

God always wants us to trust in him, regardless of any situation. We are to trust him and always keep our faith in him and not to turn away from him.

(6)

THERE ARE SIX THINGS THE LORD HATES, SEVEN ARE DETESTABLE TO HIM.

1. A HAUGHTY EYES.
2. A LYING TONGUE.
3. HANDS THAT SHED INNOCENT BLOOD.
4. A HEART THAT DEVISES WICKED SCHEMES.
5. FEET THAT ARE QUICK TO RUSH INTO EVIL.
6. A FALSE WITNESS WHO POURS OUT LIES.
7. AND A MAN WHO STIRS UP DISSENSIONS (DIVISIONS) AMONG BROTHERS. (believers).

Proverbs 6 v 16 - 19.

(7)

THE LORD HATES IT WHEN WE TRY TO FALSIFY MEASUREMENTS IN ORDER TO MAKE GAIN.

"The Lord hates dishonest scales, but accurate weights are his delight."

Proverbs 11 v 1.

"Do not use dishonest standards when measuring length, weight or quantity. Use honest scales and honest weights, an honest ephah, and an honest hin.

Leviticus 19 v 35.

Gaining wealth by deceit, falsifying records etc.

This is a fraudulent act and God is not for it.

(8)

GOD HATES THOSE WHO THINK EVIL IN THEIR HEART AGAINST THEIR NEIGHBOUR.

"And the word of the Lord came again to Zechariah, This is what the Almighty says, In your hearts do not think evil of each other."

Zechariah 7 v 10b.

"He who despises his neighbour sins."

Proverbs 14 v 21.

"Do not hate your brother in your hearts."

Leviticus 19 v 18.

"Do not do anything that endangers your neighbours life."

Leviticus 19 v 16b.

(9)

GOD HATES DIVORCE.

"I hate divorce, says the Lord."

Malachi 2 v 16.

(10)

GOD IS AGAINST US MAKING

TATOOS ON OUR BODIES.

"Do not put tattoo marks on yourself."

Leviticus 19 v 28b.

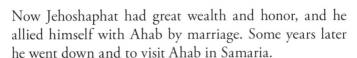

(11)

GOD COMMANDS US NOT TO SIT IN

THE COUNSEL OF THE UNGODLY.

"Blessed is the man who does not walk in the counsel of
the wicked or stand in the way of sinners."

Psalm 1v 1.

Now Jehoshaphat had great wealth and honor, and he
allied himself with Ahab by marriage. Some years later
he went down and to visit Ahab in Samaria.

When Jehoshaphat king of Judah returned safely to his
palace in Jerusalem, Jehu the seer, the son of Hanani,
went out to meet him and said to the king, **Should you
help the wicked and love those who hate the Lord?
Because of this, the wrath of the Lord is upon you.**

2nd Chron 18 v 1, 2. 19 v 1-2.

Jehoshaphat was a good man who loved the Lord and
he served the Lord wholeheartedly, however he incurred
the wrath of God because of his wrong association. He
alligned himself with king Ahab who was very evil and

an idolater. Therefore we have to be very careful, who we associate with and the steps we take. We are to walk circumspectly, because one bad egg will make a crate of 29 good eggs to bring out a bad smell.

God watches all our steps. His eyes are on our ways.

For a man's ways are in full view of the Lord, and he examines all his paths.

Prov 5 v 21.

(12)

GOD COMMANDS US NOT TO TAKE OUT VEGEANCE BY OURSELVES.

"Do not repay anyone evil for evil. Be careful to do what is right in the eyes of everybody. If it is possible, as far as it depends on you live at peace with everyone. Do not take revenge, my friends, but leave room for God's wrath, for it is written, it is mine to avenge, I will repay says the Lord. On the contrary if your enemy is hungry, feed him, if he is thirsty, give him something to drink, in doing this, you will heap burning coals on his head. Do not be overcome by evil, but overcome evil with good."

Romans 12 v 17-21.

"Do not say, I will do to him as he has done to me; I will pay that man back for what he did."

Proverbs 24 v 29.

"Do not seek revenge."

Leviticus 19 v 18.

(13)

GOD HATES IT WHEN WE TRUST IN MAN.

"This is what the Lord says;

Cursed is the one who trusts in man, who depends on flesh for his strength and whose heart turns away from the Lord. He will be like a bush in the wastelands, he will not see prosperity when it comes. He will dwell in the parched places of the desert, in a salt land where no one lives."

Jeremiah 17 v 5 - 6.

(14)

GOD HATES IT WHEN WE DOUBT HIS WORD.

"But when he asks, he must believe and not doubt, because he who doubts is like a wave of the sea, blown and tossed by the wind. That man should not think he will receive anything from the Lord. He is double-minded man, unstable in all he does."

James 1 v 6 - 8.

You can't separate God from his word. God and his word is one. In the beginning was the word and word was with God and the word was God. John 1 v 1. Everyone who comes to God must believe that he is and is a rewarder of them that diligently seeks him. Therefore we have to believe every word of God in the bible and erase every doubt. Doubt is a destiny killer, doubt will rob anyone of God's abundant blessings.

(15)

GOD WARNS AGAINST BEARING

GRUDGES.

"Do not bear grudges against one of your people, but love your neighbour as yourself."

Leviticus 19 v 10.

"Get rid of all bitterness, rage, anger, brawling and slander along with every form of malice.

Ephesians 4 v 31

໑໑໑໑໑

(16)

GOD HATES IT WHEN WE PLOT

EVIL AGAINST OUR NEIGHBOUR.

"This is what the Lord Almighty says, these are the things you are to do; Do not plot evil against your neighbour, I hate all this."

Zechariah 8 v 14a-17.

"Do not defraud your neighbour or rob him."

Leviticus 19 v 13.

"Do not do anything that endangers your neighbour's life. I am the Lord."

Leviticus 19 v 16b.

༄༄༄༄༄

---

(17)

GOD HATES HOMOSEXUALITY.

"Do not lie with a man as one lies with a woman, that is detestable."

Leviticus 18 v 22.

This is a very grievous act before the throne of God, but society has stamped it on us that it is alright. This is a sin before the eyes of God. As hard as society makes it acceptable does not mean it is right. It is immorally wrong and God frowns at it.

In Genesis 18 and 19, there was a city called Sodom and Gomorrah. The men of this city all engaged in homosexual acts. And God himself had to come down from heaven just to destroy the city.

"Then the Lord said, The outcry against Sodom and Gomorrah is so great and their sin so grievous that I will go down and see."

And God sent two angels to go ahead of him into the city. And guess what the men of the city wanted to have sex with these angelic beings.

"Then the two angels arrived Sodom and Gomorrah in the evening and Lot was sitting in the gateway of the city. When he saw them he got up and insisted they stay with him.

Before they had gone to bed, all the men from every part of the city of Sodom, both young and old surrounded the house. They called to Lot, where are the men who came to you tonight? Bring them out to us so that we can have sex with them."

And the ANGER OF THE LORD BURNED AGAINST THE CITY, and the Lord rained down burning sulphur on Sodom and Gomorrah. GOD DESTROYED THE CITY BECAUSE OF THIS LEWD ACT OF HOMOSEXUALITY.

God is still the same he has not changed, if he could come down and destroy a whole city because of homosexual acts, he will still do it again. Please we should desist from provoking the almighty God and repent from this satanic act. The devil is the founder and originator of homosexuality. The devil tries to initiate things that will take people out of God's presence. The devil stands for everything, God is against and he is against everything God stands for. The devil distorts the thinking of people by making them think it is o.k to be gay, no it is not o.k to be gay and being gay is not God's idea. In the beginning God created them male and female.

Then the Lord God made a woman, and he brought her to the man.
For this reason (why a woman was created) a man will leave his father and mother and be united to his wife (not to a fellow man) and they (man and woman) will become one flesh.
                    Gen 2 v 22, 24. Emp added

From the above we can see that indeed homosexuality is the stupid devil's idea.

Society has got it wrong on this issue. God is a God of love and mercy, he loves everyone including the homosexual but he hates the homosexual acts and he is still a God of judgement. He will judge everyone.

Men commited indecent acts with other men and received in themselves the due penalty for their pervasion.
                                        Rom 1 v 27.

(18)

GOD HATES IT WHEN WE EAT
FOOD SACRIFICED TO IDOLS.

"Nevertheless, I have this against you, you have people there who hold to the teaching of Balaam, who taught Balak to entice the Israelites to sin by eating food sacrificed to idols."

Revelation 2 v 14b 20.

"The sacrifices of pagans are offered to demons, not to God, and I do not want you to be participants with demons. You cannot drink the cup of the Lord and the cup of demons too, you cannot have a part in both the Lord's table and the table of demons."

1st Corinthians 10 v 20-22.

(19)

GOD HATES IT WHEN WE OPRESS THE POOR, WIDOW, ALIEN AND FATHERLESS.

"And the word of the Lord came again to Zechariah. This is what the Lord Almighty says; Do not oppress the widow or the fatherless, the alien or the poor".

Zechariah 7 v 8- 10.

"So I will come near to you for judgement, I will be quick to testify against those who oppress the widows and fatherless and deprive aliens of justice, but do not fear me, says the Lord Almighty."

Malachi 3 v 5.

(20)

GOD HATES COVETOUSNESS.

"You shall not covet your neighbour's house, you shall not covet your neighbour's wife, or his manservant or maidservant, his ox or donkey, or anything that belongs to your neighbour."

Exodus 20 v 17.

(21)

GOD DOES NOT STAND FOR

POLYGAMY.

"At the beginning God made them male and female and said For this reason a man will leave his father and mother and be united to HIS WIFE [NOT WIVES] and the TWO [NOT THREE OR FOUR] will become one flesh. So they are no longer two, but one."

Matthew 19 v 4 - 6. Emphasis added.

ଡ଼ଡ଼ଡ଼ଡ଼ଡ଼

(22)

GOD HATES SEXUAL PERVASION.

This is having sex the wrong way, shifting away from the natural way of sex. Such as;

(a) **Oral sex--** Having sex through the mouth organ. Do not put the male organ in the mouth and do not put your mouth in the female organ. God is an holy God and he can't stand any form of depravity that results into unholines.

(b) **Anal sex--** sex through the anus. These days, this is not secluded only to gay couples, but it is becoming rampart among straight couples (Man and woman). A lot of women have reported that their husbands also request to have sex through the anus with them. Some of them allow their husbands to do it, just to keep their home and some refuse bluntly. (What a chaotic situation).

(c) **Sex tools--** this is no news, as most women engage in sex by using a vibrator. It is so bad that even married women in their matrimonial homes engage in this illicit act.

(d) Wrong foreplay- This is a very subtle way, because most people are ignorantly guilty of this. Soceity and the world has termed it o.k for the woman to put the male organ in her mouth and also for the man to put his mouth in the female organ to arouse each other. Infact there are books and materials circulated worldwide to teach and encourage such acts. This is purely unholy, both the male and female organ is not meant to be put in the mouth.

God is an holy God. And without any apology anyone doing so should refrain from such depraved act. God made the male organ to be inserted into the female organ and the mouth for eating, talking, singing, communicating and praying, the mouth is not to be put into the female organ.

(e) Masturbation-- having sex alone, with oneself.

(f) Lesbianism- Women having affairs with their fellow women. This is utterly wrong. God is against it. In the beginning God created Adam, a man. Then he said it is not good for a man to be alone, so he created a woman for him, as a help mate, as a companion. God created the female to be with a man, and not female to stay with female, vice versa. But what do we have these days, the devil has used society as a tool to twist the truth for a lie. How can a woman lie with a woman, and a man lie with a man? This is worse than sodomy, this is pure sexual pervasion.

Woman do not be deceived, you were specially created, and endowed with natural beauty to please and be with a man. You were not created to lie and be with another woman.

I break every yoke of sodomy, lesbianism, homosexuality over the lives of people in Jesus name.

All the above is classified as unnatural ways of having sex.

This is what the almighty God says to those who engage in such acts;

"The wrath of God is being revealed from heaven against ungodliness and unrighteousness of men."

"Even their women exchanged natural relations for unnatural ones. In the same way the men also abandoned natural relations with women and were inflamed with lust for one another. **Men committed indecent acts with other men and received in themselves the due penalty for their pervasion.**

Romans 1 v 26 - 27, 32.

In as much as God is a God of mercy, he is also a God of judgement.

(23)

GOD HATES IT WHEN WE DO NOT LOOK UP TO HIM FOR HELP.

"Woe to those who go down to Egypt for help, who rely on horses, who trust in the multitude of their chariots and in the great strength of their horsemen, but do not look to the Holy one of Israel, or seek help from the Lord.

But the Egyptians are men and not God; their horses are flesh and not spirit, when the Lord stretches out his hand, he who helps will stumble, he who is helped will fall, both will perish."

Isaiah 31 v 1 - 3.

(24)

GOD IS FAR FROM WHOEVER

REPAYS EVIL FOR GOOD.

"If a man pays back evil for good, evil will never leave his house."

Proverbs 17 v 13.

(25)

GOD DISLIKES IT WHEN WE LIVE
IN UNFORGIVENESS.

"Bear with each other and forgive whatever grievances you may have against one another. Forgive as the Lord forgave you."

"Be kind and compassionate to one another, forgiving each other, just as in Christ God forgave you."

Ephesians 4 v 32.

For if you forgive men when they sin against you, your heavenly father will also forgive you. But if you do not forgive men their sins, your father will not forgive your sins.

Matthew 6 v 14.

On this issue, God has been very explicit. God warns that if we don't forgive there is no way we can receive forgiveness nor can our prayers be heard. Majority of christians are very adamant when it comes to this topic. They feel they can do things their own way by refusing to forgive those who offend them. Friends if you don't forgive, God will not hear your prayers. So what's the point of holding anyone in unforgiveness. Why cause harm to yourself. Your relationship with God is far more precious than bearing grudges and living in unforgiveness. Some people say, they forgive but don't forget. That is wickedness, how can you say you have forgiven a person, yet you still remember the offence. This is deception in the highest order. If we claim to be children of God, we have to be like our father who forgives our sins and remembers them no more.

In Matthew 18 v 23 - 35 tells of a servant who owed his master so much debt and begged for the debts to be canceled. The master forgave him. But when he went out, there was another servant who was owing him and he refused to forgive this fellow and dealt harshly with him. When the master heard he was very furious and he called the servant in. You wicked servant, I canceled all that debt of yours because you begged me to. Shouldn't you have had mercy on your fellow servant just as i had on you. In anger his master turned him over to the jailers to be tortured, until he should pay back all he owed.

This is how God will treat each of you unless you forgive your brother from your heart. Matt 18 v 35.

(26)

GOD HATES REBELLION

"For rebellion is as the sin of witchcraft."

Sam 15 v 23

Rebellion is showing disregard for God, constituted authority such as government, the church, organization, place of work, family and etc.

Saul disregarded the office of the priesthood and he went ahead and offered sacrifices.

That role was not meant for him, but he still went ahead, that was a rebellious act and God replaced him. God is a God of orderliness and we are expected to be orderly by being obedient. To obey is better than sacrifice.

So it is today, we have to be very careful, so as not to champion any cause to promote rebellion such as gossiping to other brethren, causing strife and division in the church and so on. Also we should not go about gathering storm that would constitute rebellion.

(27)

GOD HATES CONSULTING
THE DEAD. (NECROMANCY).

"Let no one be found among you who consults the dead. Anyone who does these things is detestable."

Deuteronomy 18 v 11.

I will set my face against the person who turns to mediums and spiritists to prostitute himself by following them, and i will cut him off from his people.

Lev 20 v 6.

Once a person dies, his or her soul departs this world into eternity. This could either be heaven or hell. The person's soul does not hang around as some people are made to believe.

When Jesus was crucified along with two robbers, he told the other robber, this day (that is right now, not in the future) you would be with me in paradise.

Also there is no relation between the dead and living. But traditions of men and society have made people to believe that it is o.k to communicate with dead people. God warns strongly against consulting the dead on behalf of the living because demons are being activated through such means. Necromancy is purely an extension of demonic activities. Demons impersonify the dead person and act like them. This happened in 1st Samuel 28 when King Saul consulted the witch of Endor to help him communicate with the ghost of Samuel.

The witch went ahead with his request, because she knew it would only be an impersonifying demon that would appear. But to her utmost surprise the real Samuel appeared and she was so horrified because this has never happened before.

In some parts of Europe, society has made it a trend and it is an o.k thing for people to consult the dead. Necromancy practice is the order of the day and they attach so much importance to the existence of Ghost. As a matter of fact this is a therapy for them, because when they lose a loved one they find it hard to come to terms with it, so they try to connect with the dead person. However rather than consulting with the dead, they are actually consulting and contacting demon spirits.

Because it is appointed for man to live once and after that judgment

Heb 9 v 27

This demon spirits are called Ghost and this Ghost begins to control their lives. When you engage in necromancy you open the doorway of your life and you actually invite demons into your life. These demon Ghost starts controlling and manipulating its victims.

That is why you find people that would just wake up and do abnormal and weird things, such as setting themselves ablaze or running into a moving train and all sorts.

Most victims have confessed that they keep hearing voices speaking to them. Without any apology in the western world, most people that end up in psychiatric homes are mostly victims of necromancy. Necromancy opens the doorway for demons to enter and control human beings at will,

A classical example of a life controlled by demons is found in Mark 5 v 1 - 20.

"When Jesus got out of the boat, a man with an evil spirit came from the tombs to meet him. This man lived in the tombs and no one could bind him anymore, not even with a chain. For he had often been chained hand and foot, but he tore the chains apart and broke the irons on his feet. No one was strong enough to subdue him. Night and day among the tombs and in the hills he would cry out and cut himself with stones.

When he saw Jesus he bowed before Jesus and Jesus commanded the demons to come out of him. Then Jesus asked what is your name and the demon replied saying my name is legion for we are many. And the demons begged to be sent into a large herd of pigs. He gave them permission and the evil spirits came out and went into the pigs.

V 15. When they came to Jesus, they saw the man who had been possessed by the legion of demons sitting there, dressed and in HIS RIGHT MIND and they were afraid.

Ha ha, so we can see that this mad man was simply possessed by demons. To the entire world he was mad, but in the realm of the spirit he was being controlled and influenced by demons. If it was in this modern times he will surely end up in a pyschiatric home with all sorts of highly qualified doctors carrying out different test and diagonsis on him and arriving at different medical conclusions with no visible cure. This is not mental illness, but a pure case of demon affliction.

Psychiatric doctors refer to them as mentally ill as a result of stress and try to treat them medically. The truth of the matter is that this is not a medical induced problem, but a demonically induced problem, because the victims are seeing things, hearing voices which is abnormal and are being controlled by demons.

(28)

GOD HATES MURMURING

Murmuring is an act, that signifies ingratitude. When you murmur, you are telling God he has not done enough for you. Also murmuring arouses God's anger.

'The people complained about their hardship in the hearing of the Lord and when GOD HEARD THEM, GOD'S ANGER WAS AROUSED.'

Numbers 11 v 1.

(29)

GOD WARNS AGAINST GRUMBLING

AGAINST EACH OTHER.

"Don't grumble against each other, brothers or you will be judged. The judge is standing at the door."

James 5 v 9.

෨෨෨෨෨

(30)

GOD FROWNS AT DRUNKENESS.

"Woe to those who rise early in the morning, to run after their drinks, who stay up late at night till they are inflamed with wine."

Isaiah 5 v 11.

"Woe to those are who are heroes at drinking wine and champions at mixing drinks, as tongues of fire lick up straw and as dry grass sinks down in the flames, so their roots will decay and their flowers blow away like dust; for they have rejected the law of the Lord Almighty."

Isaiah 5 v 22, 24.

God warns against drunkenness. Do not be drunk with wine, which leads to debauchery. Debauchery is a sin and it is one of the works of the flesh.

God frowns against drunkenness because,

1) Alcohol which is a fermented drink, when consumed distorts the functioning of the brain temporarily. And in that temporary state a lot can happen. You could take decisions that could be adverse or have an adverse effect on you permanently.

   An example of this is the story of Lot in, Gen 19 v 2 'Let's get our father to drink wine and then lie with him and preserve our family line through our father. That night they got their father to drink wine and the older went in and lay with him. He was not aware of it when she lay down or when she got up.

   So they got their father to drink wine the next night also, and the younger daughter went and lay with him. So both daughters became pregnant by their father.

   Therefore the destiny of Lot was altered and ruined as a result of being drunk with alcohol.

2) Do not gaze at wine when it is red, when it sparkles in the cup, when it goes down smoothly. In the end it bites like snake and poisons like a viper.
   a) Your eyes will see strange sights.
   b) Your mind imagine confusing things.
   c) You will be like one sleeping on the high seas.

"Give beer to those who are perishing, wine to those who are perishing, wine to those who are in anguish, let them drink and forget their poverty and remember their misery no more."
Proverbs 31 v 6 -7.

Also some people argue that in 1ˢᵗ Timothy 5 v 23 Paul asked Timothy to take a little wine for his stomach so it is o.k to take a little wine as long as you don't get drunk.

Well, for those who think this way should remember that the bible says, we should flee every appearance of evil. And little foxes ruin the vine-yard, also a little stench causes the oil of apothecary to bring forth a bad smell.

We should be filled with the Holy Spirit and not wine. Also our body is the temple of God and we have been made a priest unto God to serve him. And in the old testament a priest was not allowed to drink any fermented drink or alcohol.

Alcohol does not feed our spirit man, but feeds our flesh. We are not to sow to the flesh, but to the spirit.

Do not be deceived, God cannot be mocked. A man reaps what he sows. The one who sows to please the flesh will of the flesh reap destruction. The one who sows to please the Spirit will reap eternal life.

Galatians 6 v 7 - 8.

If we sow to the flesh we can't hear God or walk in the spirit. If you join with a prostitute you became one with a prostitute, therefore if you join with alcohol you became alcoholic. We are in the end times, therefore, we have to watch and pray and be ever ready for Jesus.

෨෧෨෧෨

(31)

GOD HATES ABORTION.

And for your lifeblood, i will surely demand an accounting. I will demand an accounting from every animal. And from each man too, i will demand an accounting for the life of his fellow man.

Genesis 9 v 4.

Before I formed you in the womb I knew you.

Jeremiah 1 v 5.

Every life is precious to God. God is the creator and he is the only one that has the power to start every human life. No one has the power to form or create a human life, therefore no one should have the right to terminate the life God is forming.

Some would argue that pregnancy at an earlier stage, is just merely a collection of blood, so it is O.K to terminate it since it has not formed to be a human being yet. Hear this, the word of God says in Lev 17 v 14 the

life of every living thing is in the blood. Hence it is a great sin, for anyone to terminate the process / cycle of life and God frowns at this because it is murder, the shedding of innocent blood.

No murderer shall inherit the kingdom of God. Rev 22 v 15.

৩৩৩৩৩

(32)

GOD HATES SEXUAL IMMORALITY.

"Flee all sexual immorality. All other sins a man commits are outside his body, but he who sins sexually sins against his own body. Do you not know that your body is the temple of Holy Spirit, who is in you. Therefore honour God with your body."

1st Corinthians 6 v 18.

(33)

GOD HATES WHEN WE CONSULT SORCERORS, ENGAGE IN WITCHCRAFT, SEEK MEDUIMS SEEK SPIRITIST, ENGAGE IN PALM READING, ENGAGE IN CRYSTAL BALL, STAR GAZERS DIVINATION.

"Let no one be found among you, who practices divination or sorcery, interprets omens, engages in witchcraft, or cast spells, or who is a spiritist. Anyone who does these things is detestable to the Lord."

Deuteronomy 18 v 10 - 11.

"Do not practice divination or sorcery."

Leviticus 19 v 26b.

"Do not turn to mediums or seek out spiritists, for you would be defiled by them."

Leviticus 19 v 31.

"I will set my face against the person who turns to mediums and spiritists to prostitute himself by following them."

Leviticus 20 v 6.

"So Saul died because he was unfaithful to the Lord, he did not keep the word of the Lord and even consulted a medium for guidance."

1st Chron 10 v 13

(34)

GOD DOES NOT LIKE IT WHEN WE DO NOT WALK IN LOVE.

"We know that we have passed from death to life, because we love we love our brothers. Anyone who does not love remains in death. Anyone who hates his brother is a murderer, and you know that no murderer has eternal life in him."

1st John 3 v 13 -15.

"If anyone says, I love God, yet hates his brother, he is a liar. For anyone who does not love his brother, whom he has seen, cannot love God whom he has not seen. And he has given us this command; whoever loves God must also love his brother."

1st John 4 v 19.

"Do not hate your brother in your heart."

Leviticus 19 v 17.

(35)

GOD WARNS AGAINST BOASTING.

"Now listen you who say, today or tomorrow we will go to this or that city, spend a year there, carry on business and make money. Why, you do not even know what will happen tomorrow. Instead you ought to say, if it is the Lord's will, we will live and do this or that. As it is, you boast and brag. All such boasting is evil."

James 4 v 13 -16.

(36)

GOD WARNS AGAINST WORRYING.

Therefore I tell you, do not worry about your life, what you will eat or drink or about your body, what you will wear. Is not life more important than food and the body more important than clothes. Look at the birds of the air, they do not sow or reap or store away in barns, and yet your heavenly father feeds them. Are you not much more valuable than they? Who of you by worrying can add a single hour to his life.

Matthew 6 v 25-27

Worrying signifies an act of faithlessness. The bible clearly emphasizes that we should walk by faith and not by sight. Friends if you keep looking at prevailing circumstances you will start to worry. As long as Peter kept his eyes on Jesus he could walk on water, but the moment he took his eyes of Jesus and started worrying about the storms and the contrary winds blowing against him, he started to sink.

Please always bear in mind that as long as you live in this world, there will always be challenges, but you have to learn not to worry about them, but to always look unto Jesus the author and finisher of your faith.

And also bear in mind that one of the names of God is JEHOVAH THE ALL SUFFICIENT ONE. God is more than enough to meet and have all your needs met, so hold on to him.

(37)

GOD IS AGAINST SUICIDE.

For every living soul belongs to me, the father as well as the son, both alike belong to me.

Ezekiel 18 v 4.

No one, owns his or her own life. Every life is owned by God, therefore no one has a right to take his or her own life. This is a sin and God frowns at it. Anyone who commits suicide can be classified as a murderer and the bible says no murderer shall inherit the kingdom of God.

(38)

GOD FROWNS AT BACKSLIDDING.

"For in just a little while, he who is coming will come and will not delay, But my righteous one will live by faith. And if HE SHRINKS BACK (Backslide) I WILL NOT BE PLEASED WITH HIM."

Hebrew 10 v 38

(39)

GOD HATES IT WHEN WE SWEAR

FALSELY.

"Do not love to swear falsely, I hate all this, declares the Lord Almighty."

Zechariah 8 v 17.

"Do not swear falsely by my name and so profane the name of your God. I am the Lord."

Leviticus 19 v 12.

෨෩෨෩෨

(40)

GOD DOES NOT WANT US TO BE
EQUALLY YOKED WITH UNBELIEVERS.

"Do not be yoked together with unbelievers. For what do righteousness and wickedness have in common? Or what fellowship can light have with darkness? What harmony is there between Christ and Belial? What does a believer have in common with an unbeliever?

What agreement is there between the temple of God and idols? For we are the temple of the living God. As God has said, I will live with them and walk among them, and I will be their God and they will be my people. THEREFORE COME OUT FROM THEM AND BE SEPERATE."

2nd Corinthians 6 v 14 - 17.

(41)

GOD IS AGAINST EATING MEAT WITH BLOOD.

"Any Israelite or any alien living among you who eats blood, I will set my face against that person. When you hunt an animal or bird that may be eaten you must drain out the blood and cover it with earth, because the life of every creature is its blood"

Leviticus 17 v 10, 13 - 14.

෴෴෴

(42)

GOD HATES IT WHEN WE DEFRAUD LABOURERS OF THEIR WAGES.

"Do not defraud your neighbour or rob him, do not hold back the wages of a hired man overnight."

Leviticus 19 v 13.

"So I will come near to you for judgement; I will be quick to testify against those who defraud labourers of their wages."

Malachi 3 v 5.

"Do not hold back the wages of a hired man overnight."

Leviticus 19 v 15.

಄಄಄಄

(43)

GOD FROWNS AT THOSE WHO ARE HEARERS OF THE WORD, BUT NOT DOERS OF THE WORD.

Do not merely listen to the word, and so deceive yourselves. Do what it says. Anyone who listens to the word but does not do what it says is like a man who looks at his face in the mirror and after looking at himself, goes away and immediately forgets what he looks like.
But the man who looks intently into the perfect law that gives freedom and continues to do this, not forgetting what he has heard, but doing it, will be blessed in what he does.

James 1 v 22 - 25.

Therefore everyone who hears these words of mine and puts them into practice is like a wise man who built his house on the rock. The rain came down, the streams rose and the winds blew and beat against that house, yet it did not fall, because it had it's foundation on the rock.

But everyone who hears these words of mine and does not put them into practice is like a foolish man who built his house on sand. The rain came down, the streams rose and the winds blew and beat against that house and it fell with a great crash.

Matthew 7 v 24 - 27.

(44)

GOD WARNS US NOT TO COMMIT MURDER.

"You shall not murder."

Exodus 20 v 13.

෨෨෨෨

(45)

GOD FROWNS AT ANYONE WHO DOES NOT PREPARE FOR ETERNITY.

God has set eternity in the hearts of men.

Eccle 3 v 11.

Be dressed ready for service, keep your lamps burning, like men waiting for their master to return from a wedding banquet, so that when he comes and knocks they can immediately open the door for him.

Luke 12 v 35 - 36.

God sent Jesus his only begotten Son into the world that anyone who believes in him should not **perish, but have eternal life. John 3 v 16.** It is not the desire of God that anyone should perish, that is why he made provision ahead of time. God expects everyone to utilise the gift of salvation and cash in on it to gain eternal life.

God does not wish that anyone should perish but everyone to come to repentance. 2nd Peter 3 v 9.

Therefore it saddens God's heart when people do not come to repentance nor live in readiness for heaven. Heaven is real, hell is real. No one has a choice over death, but everyone has a choice where to spend eternity. The choice and power is in your hands, therefore choose life that you may live and spend eternity in heaven with your maker. Hell is a place marked for the devil and the fallen angels. It is not meant for human beings, but unfortunately the devil has been able to drag a lot of people there with him.

Jesus shed his blood for everyone and when he was leaving this world, he assured us that in his father's house they were many mansions and that he was going to prepare a place for us in heaven. **Friends there is a place waiting for you, a mansion to be precise specially prepared for you, therefore live your life daily in anticipation that you have a place waiting for you. More so God frowns when we take this lightly and live unprepared.**

There are 5 categories of how a person can live unprepared.

1). **These are those who reject the truth of the gospel out rightly.**
This first category of people out rightly reject the truth that God exist. We can term them as atheist. But God clearly says that there is no excuse for them, and the scripture in Rom 1 v 20 confirms the mind of God.

For since the creation of the world God's invisible qualities, his eternal power and divine nature have been clearly seen, being understood from what has been made,(example the Sun, the moon, the mighty ocean, the various kinds of animals and nature as whole) so that men are without excuse.

Rom 1 v 20. Emphasis added.

2). **Those who deny the power of cross.**

The second category are some who believe that God exist, they claim to know God, but refuse to accept the finished work of the cross of Calvary. They deny the power of the cross and claim that they can earn their salvation without Jesus. The people responsible for these are so called Christian denomination, such as Jehovah witness sect, Seventh day Adventist, The church of the latter day saints, Brotherhood of the cross and star and a whole lot. These have a frame of godliness but they deny the power of the cross. And preach to their members that they have to work to earn their salvation.

The bible is clear on this issue and has clarified it in Acts 4 v 12 *Salvation is found in no one else, for there is no other name under heaven given to men by which we must be saved.*

Jesus answered,I am the way the truth and the life. No one comes to the father except through me.

John 14 v 6.

3). **Those who harden their heart and refuse to repent.**

These third category are people, who hear the word, listen to sermons, watch people that are saved, but for some reasons just refuse to repent. They are so hardened in their spirit and mind and on their own shut their hearts. They feel they are self righteous, they also feel their good works will take them far. They wallow in self deception. They are like the Pharisees, who saw Jesus, heard him, witnessed all the miracles, yet they hardened their minds and hearts and just refuse to repent. We have a lot of modern day Pharisees.

Likewise we have a lot of people who are modern day example of the Rich ruler in Luke 18 v 18 -23. He went to Jesus to ask how he can earn eternal life, and Jesus told him what to do. One would have thought that he would jump for joy but he turned down the offer that would make him to earn eternal life and walked away. He preferred to enjoy his wealth and the pleasures of this world than to gain eternal life. Its really strange, how a person will turn down such an offer, but beloved the truth is, this is real and it is happening in this day and age we live in, people for some reason just refuse salvation.

What good is it for a man to gain the whole world and loose his soul, or what will a man give in exchange for his soul.

Mark 8 v 36 -37.

4). **Those who accept Jesus into their lives but they continue to live in sin.**

The bible says in Rom 6 v 1, shall we continue in sin that grace may abound. Certainly no, we died to sin, how can we live in it.
Also God has given us the grace to live above sin.

For the grace of God that brings salvation has appeared to all men. It teaches us to say no to ungodliness and worldly passions and to live self controlled, upright and godly lives in this present age.

Titus 2 v 11.

If you have accepted Jesus into your life, you are not expected to carry on living in sin. Sin is a cankerworm and it will rob you of your glorious destiny and place in heaven. Beloved on this issue we have to be very careful, because there are some men of God who preach that ONCE SAVED FOREVER SAVED. THIS PREACHING IS A LIE FROM THE PIT OF HELL. God is a holy God and we have to serve him in truth and holiness.

If we deliberately keep on sinning after we have received the knowledge of truth, no sacrifice for sins is left, but only a fearful expectation of judgement and a raging fire that will consume the enemies of God. (Heb 10 v 26- 27).

Do you know that the wicked will not inherit the kingdom of God? Do not be deceived, neither the sexually immoral nor idolaters nor adulterers nor male prostitutes nor homosexuals offenders, nor thieves nor the greedy nor drunkards nor slanderers nor swindlers will inherit the kingdom of God.

1st Corinthians 6 v 9.

5). **Those who have been saved, but later on backslide.**

Under this fifth category we have 3 types.

Type (A).

These are those who get saved, but for some reason backslide. Well to such people there is still room for them to be restored as long as they are alive and ask God for mercy. God will surely have mercy on them.

Type (B).

These are those who when they got saved went deep with God. Example are ministers of God and Christians who grew to spiritual maturity. These category of people have tasted of the powers of the world to come. Unfortunately when such people backslide it is impossible for them to be restored. However, there is room for forgiveness for them.

This calls for great attention and serious awareness.

It is impossible (never possible) for those who were once enlightened and have tasted the heavenly gift and have become partakers of the Holy Spirit and have tasted the good word of God and the powers of the age to come, if they fall away to renew them again to repentance since they crucify again for themselves the Son of God and put him to open shame.

Heb 6 v 4.

Type (C)

These are people who have accepted Jesus as their Lord and saviour, they love God, serve God, however suddenly they backslide and they deny the very God that they once served and speak against the power of God (that is the Holy Spirit). These people can be referred to as apostate. Apostasy is a terrible state to be in. An apostate denies the trinity, denies the birth, death and resurrection of Jesus and speaks callously against it. The whole gospel is centered on these 3. Unfortunately these category of people can not receive forgiveness, nor be restored back.

And so I tell you, every sin and blasphemy will be forgiven men, but the blasphemy against the Holy Spirit will not be forgiven. Anyone who speaks a word against the Son of Man will be forgiven, but anyone who speaks against the Holy Spirit will not be forgiven, either in this age or in the age to come.

Matt 12 v 31 - 32.

Jesus is coming and this will be sudden, no one knows the day and hour so we have to live prepared. Be dressed ready for service and keep your lamps burning.

Luke 12 v 35.

(46)

GOD WARNS AGAINST MAKING A VOW AND NOT FULFILLING IT.

Do not be quick with your mouth, do not be hasty in your heart to utter anything before God. When you make a vow to God, do not delay in fulfilling it. He has no pleasure in fools, fulfil your vow. It is better not to vow than to make a vow to and not fulfil it.

Do not let your mouth lead you into sin. And do not protest to the temple messenger, my vow was a mistake. Why should God be angry at what you say and destroy the work of your hands. Stand in awe of God.

Eccle 5 v 2 - 7.

(47)

GOD FROWNS AT SWEARING.

"Above all, my brothers do not swear, not by heaven or by earth or by anything else. Let your "Yes" be "Yes" and your "No" be "No" or you will be condemned."

James 5 v 12.

"Do not swear at all, either by heaven, for it is God's throne, or by the earth, for it is his footstool. And do not swear by your head, for you cannot make even one hair white or black. Simply let your Yes be Yes and your No, No, anything beyond this comes from the evil one."

Matthew 5 v 34 - 37.

෧෩෩෩

(48)

GOD FROWNS WHEN WE DO NOT BEAR FRUITS.

"I am the true vine, and my father is the gardener. He cuts off every branch in me that bears no fruit."

John 15 v 1-2.

(49)

GOD DETEST THE THOUGHTS OF

THE WICKED.

91 "Woe to those who plan iniquity, to those who plot evil on their beds."

Micah 2 v 1.

"I hate evil behaviour and perverse speech."

Proverbs 8 v 13c.

"Be sure of this the wicked will not go unpunished."

proverbs 11 v 21.

"A man can't be established through wickedness."

Proverbs 12 v 3.

"Yet the because the wicked do not fear God, it will not go well with them and their days will not lengthen like a shadow."

Ecclesiates 8 v 13.

(50)

GOD HATES IT WHEN WE DO NOT HONOUR HIM.

A son honors his father, and a servant his master. If I am a father, where is the honour due me? If i am a master, where is the respect due me? says the Lord Almighty.

Malachi 1 v 6.

(51)

GOD DOES NOT WANT US TO

JUDGE ONE ANOTHER.

Anyone who speaks against his brother or judges him, speaks against the law and judges it. When you judge the law you are not keeping it, but sitting in judgment on it. There is only one lawgiver and Judge, the one who is able to save and destroy. But you who are you to judge your neighbour.

James 4 v 11-12.

Do not judge, or you too will be judged, for in the same way you judge others, you will be judged and with the same measure you use it will be measured to you.

Matthew 7 v 1 - 2.

(52)

GOD DOES NOT LIKE

LUKEWARMNESS. (Neither hot nor cold).

"These are the words of the Amen, the faithful and true witness, the ruler of God's creation. I know your deeds, that you are neither cold nor hot. I wish you were either one or the other. So because you are LUKEWARM, NEITHER HOT NOR COLD, I AM ABOUT TO SPIT YOU OUT OF MY MOUTH."

Revelation 3 v 14 - 16.

(53)

GOD FROWNS AT MAKING
INCISIONS FOR THE DEAD.

"Do not cut your bodies for the dead."

Leviticus 19 v 28.

⊙⊙⊙⊙⊙

(54)

GOD HATES IT WHEN WE
SLANDER/BACKBITE.

"Whoever slanders his neighbour in secret, him will I put to silence."

Psalm 101 v 5.

"Do not go about spreading slander among your people."

Leviticus 19 v 16.

"A man who lacks judgement derides his neighbour, but a man of understanding holds his tongue."

proverbs 11 v 12.

(55)

GOD FROWNS AT

UNTHANKFULNESS / INGRATITUDE.

One of them when he saw he was healed, came back, praising God in a loud voice. He threw himself at Jesus feet and **thanked Jesus.** Jesus asked, were not all ten cleansed? Where are the other nine. **Was no one found to return and give praise to God** except this foreigner.

Luke 17 v 17.

God loves a thankful heart, and God frowns at an unthankful heart. At all times we have to maintain a grateful attitude. The intriguing thing about thankfulness is that the moment you cease to be thankful, murmuring steps in. Nature abhors vacuum.

And God really frowns at murmuring. Most of the children of Israel never made it into the promised land due to murmuring.

Rom 1 v 21 states the consequences of unthankfulness,

For although they knew God, they neither glorified him as God nor give **thanks to him. Therefore God gave them over in the sinful desires of their hearts.**

So if we don't give God thanks, God will surely give us over to the desires of our heart. This is very dicey, because the human heart is deceitful above all things and beyond cure. Who can understand it? (Jer 17 v 9.)

(56)

GOD DOES NOT LIKE FALSE WITNESSES.

"You shall not give false testimony against your neighbour."
Exodus 20 v 16.

"Do not testify against your neighbour without cause, or use your lips to deceive."

Proverbs 24 v 28.

"A false witness is deceitful."

Proverbs 14 v 25.

"A false witness will not go unpunished and he who pours out lies will perish."

Proverbs 19 v 9.

(57)

GOD HATES A PERVERSE HEART

"Men of perverse heart shall be far from me, I will have nothing to do with evil."

Psalm 101 v 4.

"For the Lord detest a perverse man, but takes the upright into confidence."

Proverbs 3 v 29.

"The Lord detest men of perverse heart."

Proverbs 11 v 20.

(58)

GOD HATES INJUSTICE.

"Do not pervert justice, do not show partiality to the poor or favouritism to the great, but judge your neighbour fairly.

"Leviticus 19 v 15.

ꙮꙮꙮ

(59)

GOD DOES NOT WANT ANYONE TO MISUSE HIS NAME.

You shall not misuse the name of the Lord thy God, for the Lord will not hold anyone guiltless who misuses his name.

Exodus 20 v 7.

For I am a great king, says the Lord Almighty, and my name is to be feared among the nations.

Malachi 1 v 14c.

God is an holy God, and at all given times we must show him reverence. We must stand in awe of God's name. Some people take God's name for granted and use it anyhow, even to commit fraud and tell lies.

(60)

GOD HATES IT WHEN WE WALK CARNALLY / AFTER THE FLESH.

"Now the mind of the flesh [which is sense and reason without the Holy Spirit] is death. But the mind of the Spirit is life and peace.[That is] because the mind of the flesh [with its carnal thoughts and purposes] is hostile to God, for it does not submit itself to God's law, indeed it cannot."

Romans 8 v 6 - 7. Amp bible.

"The carnal mind is enmity with God.

Romans 8 v

Carnality is living to please the flesh and living without the Spirit of God. Carnality negates the very purpose why God created us. In the beginning God created man clean and holy, but the devil came to sow the seed of carnality and thus caused a seperation between God and man.

However Jesus came to restore man back to God, back to the heart of worship, back to fellowship and intimacy with God. So man is without excuse, therefore we are all expected to live after the Spirit and not after the flesh.

God frowns at any christian who still lives carnally and walk after the flesh. God is a Spirit and all his worshipers must worship in truth and spirit. (John 4 v 23).

The carnal mind can't understand the things of God because they are spiritually discerned. To be carnally minded is death, but to be spiritually minded is life and peace.

(61)

GOD FROWNS AT ADULTERY.

"Thou shall not commit adultery.

Exodus 20 v 14.

No adulterer shall inherit the kingdom of God.

"The prostitutes reduces you to a loaf of bread, and the adulteress preys upon your very life. Can a man scoop fire into his lap without his clothes being burned. Can a man walk on hot coals without being scorched? So is he who sleeps with another man's wife, no one who touches her will unpunished.

A man who commits adultery lacks judgement, whoever does so destroys himself."

Proverbs 6 v 26-29, 32.

(62)

GOD HATES STEALING.

"Thou shall not steal."

Exodus 20 v 15.

"Do not steal."

Leviticus 19 v 11.

"A thief must certainly make restitution."

Exodus 22 v 3.

(63)

GOD DISLIKES IT WHEN WE PRACTICE DECEIT.

"No one who practices deceit will dwell in my house, no one who speaks falsely will stand in my presence."

Psalm 101 v 7.

"You destroy those who tell lies, bloodthirsty and deceitful men, the Lord abhors."

Psalm 5 v 6.

(64)

THE FACE OF THE LORD IS AGAINST THE WICKED/EVILDOERS.

"The Lord's curse is on the house of the wicked."

Proverbs 3 v 33.

"The Lord detest the way of the wicked."

Proverbs 15 v 9.

"You are not a God who takes pleasure in evil, with you the wicked cannot dwell. The arrogant cannot stand in your presence. You hate all who do wrong."

Psalm 5 v 4 - 5.

(65)

GOD FROWNS AT THOSE WHO DO NOT FEAR HIM.

We are not to fear man, but we are only to fear God.

"Who are you that you fear mortal men, the sons of men who are but grass, that you forget your Maker, who stretched out the heavens and laid the foundations of the earth

༄༄༄༄༄

(66)

GOD'S WARNING IN REGARDS TO UNLAWFUL SEXUAL RELATIONS.

"The Lord said to Moses, speak to the Israelites and say to them; I am the Lord your God. You must not do as they do in Egypt, do not follow their practices. You must obey my laws and be careful to follow my decrees.

I am the Lord your God. Keep my decrees and law, for the man who obeys them will live by them. I am the Lord.

No one is too approach any close relative to have sexual relations. Leviticus 18 v 1-5.

(a) "No one is to approach any close relative to have sexual relations."

Leviticus 18 v 6.

(b) "Do not dishonour your father by having sexual relations with your mother. She is your mother, do not have relations with her."

Leviticus 18 v 7.

(c) "Do not have sexual relations with your father's wife, that would dishonour your Father."

Leviticus 18 v 8.

(d) "Do not have sexual relations with your sister, either your father's daughter or your mother's daughter, whether she was born in the same home or elsewhere."

Leviticus 18 v 9.

(e) "Do not have sexual relations with your son's daughter or your daughter's daughter that would dishonour you."

Leviticus 18 v 10.

(f) "Do not have sexual relations with the daughter of your father's wife, born to your father, she is your sister."

Leviticus 18 v 11.

(g) "Do not have sexual relations with your father's sister, she is your father's close relative."

Leviticus 18 v 12.

(h) "Do not have sexual relations with your mother's sister, because she is your mother's close relative."

Leviticus 18 v 13.

(i) "Do not dishonour your father's brother by approaching his wife to have sexual relations, she is your aunt."

Leviticus 18 v 14.

(j) "Do not have sexual relations with our daughter in law. She is your son's wife, do not have relations with her."

Leviticus 18 v 15.

(k) "Do not have sexual have sexual relations with your brother's wife, that would dishonour your brother."

Leviticus 18 v 16.

(l) "Do not have sexual relations with both a woman and her daughter. Do no have sexual relations with either her son's daughter or her daughter's daughter, they are close relatives. That is wickedness.

Leviticus 18 v 17.

(m) "Do not take your wife's sister as a rival wife and have sexual relations with her while your wife is still living."

Leviticus 18 v 18.

(n) "Do not approach a woman to have sexual relations during the uncleanness of her monthly period."

Leviticus 18 v 19

(o) "Do not have sexual relations with your neighbour's wife and defile yourself with her."

Leviticus 18 v 20.

"Do not defile yourself in any of these ways, Everyone who does any of these detestable things such persons must be cut off from their people."

Leviticus 18 v 29.

(67)

GOD HATES THOSE WHO GIVE BRIBES AND THOSE WHO ACCEPT BRIBES.

"Do not accept a bribe, for a bribe blinds those who see and twists the words of the righteous."

Exodus 23 v 8.

"Woe to those who acquit the guilty for a bribe, but deny justice to the innocent. Therefore as tongues of fire lick up straw and as dry grass sinks like down in flames, so their roots will decay and their flowers blow away like dust."

Isaiah 5 v 23 -24.

(68)

GOD WARNS ABOUT CARELESS SPEECHES.

"But I tell you that men will have to give account on the day of judgement for every careless word they have spoken. For by your words you will be acquitted, and by your words you will be condemned."

Matthew 12 v 36.

"Let each one be quick to listen, slow to speak and slow to became angry."

James 1 v 19.

(69)

GOD FROWNS WHEN WE HATE

OUR ENEMIES.

"You have heard that it was said, Love your neighbour and hate your enemy. But I tell, love your enemies and pray for those who persecute you, that you maybe sons of your father in heaven.

He causes his sun to rise on the evil and the good, and sends rain on the righteous and the unrighteous.

If you love those who love you, what reward will you get. Are not even the tax collectors doing that. And if you greet only your brothers, what are you doing more than others. Do not even pagans do that. Be perfect, therefore as your heavenly father is perfect."

Matthew 5 v 43 - 48.

(70)

GOD FROWNS WHEN WE REJOICE OVER THE DOWNFALL OF OUR ENEMIES.

"Do not gloat when your enemy falls, when he stumbles, do not let your heart rejoice, or the Lord will see and disapprove and turn his wrath away from him."

Proverbs 24 v 17.

Epilogue

Lord who may dwell in your sanctuary? who may live on your holy hill,

He whose walk is blameless, and does what is righteous,

Who speaks the truth from his heart

And has no slander on his tongue

Who does his neighbour no wrong

And cast no slur on his fellowman

Who despises a vile man

But honours those who fear the lord

Who keeps his oath even when it hurts

Who lends his money without usury

And who does not accept a bribe against the innocent.

He who does these things will never be shaken.

Psalm 15 v 1 - 5.

Printed in the United States
By Bookmasters